ISLAM ISRAEL AND THE LAST DAYS

Elishua Davidson

HARVEST HOUSE PUBLISHERS
Eugene, Oregon 97402

ISLAM, ISRAEL AND THE LAST DAYS

Copyright © 1991 by Sjofar
Published by Harvest House Publishers
Eugene, Oregon 97402

First published in The Netherlands in 1987, under the title *Wie Is God* (Who Is God)—
    by Elishua Davidson
ISBN 90-800159-1-1/CIP

Library of Congress Cataloging-in-Publication Data

Davidson, E.
        Islam, Israel and the last days / E. Davidson.
        Includes bibliographical references.
        ISBN 0-89081-893-2
        1. Islam—Relations—Christianity.   2. Christianity and other religions—
    Islam.   I. Title.
    BP172.D378   1991   91-4508
    297'.1972—dc20   CIP

Printed in the United States of America.

*I dedicate this book to my people the Jews,
and to Israel and Jerusalem.
I also dedicate it to the glory of God,
whose Word inspired me to write,
and whose Name will surely save.*

Contents

Foreword

I first visited Jerusalem in 1971. I was deeply affected by the tensions arising out of the conflict between Judaism, Christianity, and Islam—three religions which seemed to have so much in common, yet were actually so far apart.

While I was in Jerusalem I had a conversation with a faithful Muslim. I spoke to a Jewish Bible teacher who had spent 30 years in Morocco among both Jews and Muslims. I also talked with a rabbi, and with a Christian professor who was an authority on Islam. I had discussions, too, with an Arab Israeli pastor who had a love for Israel, and for her people and their cause. All of them raised questions in my mind.

The most important question was this: If Jews, Christians, and Muslims each believed in one and the same God, why was there so much dissension between them? Where did the truth really lie?

On the surface it might look as though Jews and Muslims have a common heritage, since both appear to believe in the God of Abraham and seem to have similar views about Jesus. We shall be considering whether this is really so. As far as Christians and Muslims are concerned, they have fundamental differences in their beliefs about Jesus.

It is commonly believed that Jesus is responsible for the separation between Judaism and Christianity,* but as long as we continue to use these two terms, this separation will persist. The Bible presents us with faith founded on divine revelation, and when from that revelation Jews and Christians discover who Jesus *really* is, they may be surprised to find that He is the One who actually unites them.

---

* See Notes regarding the use of the term "Christianity."[1]

It is written, *"The Scripture cannot be broken"* (John 10:35). The "break" between the Old and New Testaments is an artificial one. The real division is between Jews and Christians on the one hand, and Muslims on the other.

God has spoken. In order to know Him, we must study His Word. I have taken the following Scriptures as my guide:

> *The ordinances of the LORD are true . . . more to be desired are they than gold . . .*
>
> *. . . search the scriptures . . .*
>
> *Test all things; hold fast what is good.*

My aim in this book is not to give an exhaustive study of Islam; instead, just as a goldsmith needs only a small sample in order to test the purity of his metal, so I have taken some of the quranic texts and tested them against the "gold standard" of the Bible.

The Bible is the Word of God for both Jew and Christian. The Qur'an (known to many readers as the Quran or the Koran) is the sacred book of the Muslims. I have compared key texts on fundamental issues in both of them in order to assess their compatibility. I then go on to question whether the Bible and the Qur'an are inspired by one and the same person. Is the God of the Bible the same as Allah of the Qur'an?

This book is written for those Christians who believe that the faith of Jews, Christians, and Muslims can be traced back to the God of Abraham but who nevertheless find themselves confronted by many unanswered questions. Sadly, these same Christians often lack sufficient knowledge of God and His Word to be able to discern the real issue.

The book is also a cry of "Woe unto you!" to those Christian theologians who by means of "dialogue" are seeking to unite Judaism, Christianity, and Islam within one fold. In so doing they are misleading many sincere people and are undermining the authority of the Bible. Moreover, their determination to reconcile wholly incompatible beliefs shows poor respect for Muslims, when they are described as "almost-Christians, since they believe in the same God."

In writing this book my purpose has not been to seek to convince Muslims of biblical truth, since only the Word of God can do that. Many Muslims are genuinely religious and are sincerely devoted to their cause and to Allah. But when we take our stand on the truth of the Bible, it is impossible for us to call the Qur'an the truth as well.

I have read with great pleasure what J. Verkuyl and H. Kohlbrugge have written on this whole subject, and I am delighted that they echo my own thoughts on the uniqueness of the Bible. In particular, I value Verkuyl's plea for the need to make this same, unique Bible known to the Muslims, and I am indebted to Kohlbrugge for expressing the extent of the distortion which Islam imputes to biblical truth. It is here that we see two mutually exclusive and opposing powers brought face-to-face with one another, with all that this implies for Israel, her neighbors, and the world.

Finally, I want to thank all those friends who have given me so much help and support in bringing this book to birth. I am particularly grateful to Aily, Gemma, Jeremy, and Tom for their help with the work of translation and with all the final stages of the publication of this English edition. In their commitment to this whole project they have given generously of their time, energy, and love.

—Elishua Davidson
Jerusalem
Shavuot, 1990

THE MIDDLE EAST

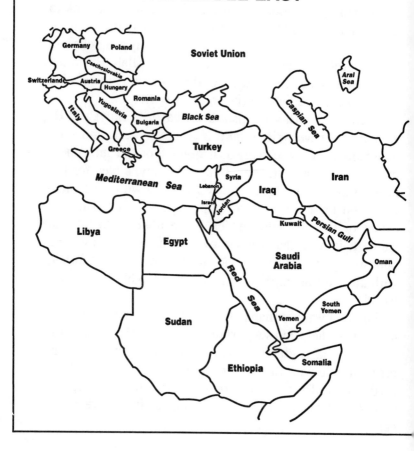

1

Already at War

##

*T*he next world war began a long time ago! At this very moment we are in the last phase of the battle being waged between the kingdom of God, the God of the Bible, and the kingdom of darkness.

Man's first attempt to go it alone in the one-world system of Babylon ended in failure (Genesis 11:1-9). Since then there has been an ever-increasing momentum toward setting up the new world order. Look closely at the back of a one-dollar bill, where are stamped the words *novus ordo seclorum* ("new order of the ages"). Throughout history people have sought to establish kingdoms and systems of government based on ideologies designed to usher in a better world, a "new age." Civilizations and Utopian dreams come and go, only to be replaced by others. World leaders are saying that by whatever means, Paradise Lost must become Paradise Regained. The slogan is: "This time it will be different; a New Age is dawning."

Will this "paradise" turn out to be a fool's paradise? Is all the turmoil going on in the Middle East right now the prelude to a Third World War? Have the aims of Communism been finally done away with? Why has the Middle East, particularly since 1973 (when the price of oil boomed), been receiving vast quantities of weaponry from the West? What is going on when the technology for waging chemical warfare is being sent by a section of German industry to one of Israel's archenemies? Are such happenings merely coincidences? And why is the nation of Israel, even its very existence, so often seen as a threat to world peace? Is the war we are involved in merely being fought in the Middle East, or will it eventually erupt in our own backyard?

What is certain is that "wars and rumors of wars" are abounding, usually in someone else's part of the world. It is easy to forget that, whether we like it or not, we are all involved in a war which is both visible and invisible.

The *Jerusalem Post* reported in its November 18, 1990 edition, that during the Gulf crisis a hundred American servicemen turned to the Islamic faith. The same article pointed out that in the United States, "in another few years Islam will be the third-largest religious denomination, replacing Judaism, which has held that place since the 1880's."

From the Archives of the Central Institute for Islamic Affairs in Germany we learn that the number of Muslims in Germany, now 1.7 million, will be 2.2 million around the year 2000, a growth of 30 percent! The expectation is that by the end of this century 33.8 percent of the world's inhabitants will be followers of Islam.

In the above-mentioned article in the *Jerusalem Post* ("Christianity's Retreat in the Mideast") Joshua Adler notes that in Britain, "... where there were only 150 mosques about 10 years ago, there are now over 1100."

Do not these facts show us that we are indeed already in the midst of a war?

My aim in writing this book is to place what is happening in the world today in its biblical context. Although I am dealing particularly with Islam, I would like to point out that this worldwide faith has much in common with Roman Catholicism. Both believe in the "one true God." Whether this "God" is indeed the same as the God of the Bible remains to be seen. The aim of both religions is to return to the ultimate goal of "one world, one people, one religion"—the old Babylonian system.

I shall first of all be concentrating on what lies behind events in the Middle East. These have already been affecting us for a long time, and too many of us are failing to realize their true significance.

The World of Islam

The word "Islam" means "submission." The ultimate aim of Islam is to make one *umma* of the people of the world, an Islamic people in submission to Allah.

Islam sees the world as being divided into two parts. That which is "in submission" is called Dar-al-Salaam (House of Peace). That which is not yet in submission is called Dar-al-Harb (House of War). To put it another way, those of us in the West who have not yet been brought into "submission" are subject to *Jihad*. This term does not simply mean the subjection of unbelievers to some kind of violent confrontation; Jihad implies everything which furthers the cause of Allah.

In recent years many Muslims have immigrated to Western countries. In a series called "What Do Muslims Believe?" broadcast over the BBC World Service in November 1990, it was explained by an Islamic spokesman that Islam also conceives of a "third domain," an "area of agreement" or political compromise.

While they remain in a minority in this domain, Muslims are advised by the Qur'an that they may gently confront people with the teachings of Islam by speaking kindly with unbelievers. This is why the inhabitants of the Western world are suddenly seeing themselves surrounded by mosques. From these, Islam can peacefully introduce its religion and culture into its adopted countries.

Many local churches in the West enter into "dialogue" with Muslims. While we must offer them our friendship and hospitality, Christian leaders need to ask themselves how many churches Islam allows to be built in countries which are exclusively Islamic.

By and large the West does not see this quiet, unaggressive approach by Islam as presenting anything much to worry about. This might be understandable, but what is almost incredible is the sheer indifference of many people in the churches to what is really going on. This is where the heart of the problem lies.

This attitude toward Islam is based not only on ignorance of the true facts about Islam's final aim, but also on the deliberate choice by so much of Christendom to shrug its shoulders and maintain that "in the end, all roads lead to the same God; after all, Muslims worship the one God too, so their God and ours must be one and the same."

What the Word Says

It is unbelievable that so many in the church no longer accept the authority of the Bible. When we ignore the Scriptures we miss out on the whole plan of God for the world. In our blindness we no longer see the deceptions which surround us on every side. We do not see the ultimate aim of Islam, nor do we realize that the world is heading for a final battle between God and the forces of evil. Many people remain ignorant of the Word of God because they have turned instead to human wisdom and the traditions of men (Mark 7:13). Among many Christians, the prophetic Scriptures have been labeled "best left alone," and the churches remain largely ignorant of what God has revealed about things to come.

Unfortunately, many Christians live almost exclusively by the New Testament, and they spiritualize nearly everything in the Old. The whole world of the Middle East, with its Jews and Muslims, has become shrouded in mystery, tucked away somewhere in a part of the world which is geographically remote. And the idea that the Lord Himself will return to this very land is just as remote from the minds of many believers (Zechariah 14:3,4; Acts 1:11).

The world's leaders and many Christian leaders talk of "peace on earth" while the Bible reminds us of those who say "Peace, peace!" when there is no peace (Jeremiah 6:14; cf. 1 Thessalonians 5:1-4). It is when people persist in resisting God's truth that He will *"send them a strong delusion, that they should believe the lie"* (2 Thessalonians 2:11).

Based on the teachings of many of the church Fathers of the third and fourth centuries, there is a widespread belief within Christendom that God is finished with the Jews.

Faulty exegesis of the biblical promises concerning all the "descendants of Abraham" has led many Christians astray. Having had little teaching on the prophetic Scriptures, they are extremely confused about the whole meaning of God's dealing with the Jews.

However, when these same believers become truly grounded in the Word of God, they sooner or later begin to have a heart for the Jewish people. They then realize that God is not finished with the Jews, and that there are still many promises for them and for the Arabs which have yet to be fulfilled. But when we come to speak about promises to the Arabs, we must remember that these were given to their forefather Ishmael.

God promised Abraham that Ishmael would become a great people (Genesis 17:20). It is clear that this promise has been kept. In the same way, there are promises for the Arabs which have yet to be fulfilled (Isaiah 19:18-25).

Sadly, Ishmael's descendants did not remain faithful to his God, the God of Abraham. Instead, they went their own way, and by the time Muhammad came on the scene they had 365 "gods." Muhammad chose one of these, Allah, to be "the one true God," whom he considered to be the giver of the promises of Ishmael.

Now, the fulfillment of promises can only be expected to come from the giver of the promises.

So Allah and the God of Abraham, Isaac, and Jacob must be one and the same. But are they?

2

Conflict in
the Middle East

*L*ance Lambert has stated eloquently
in a lecture on Israel and the nations:

"In any consideration of the whole question of Israel and
the Middle East, the most important issue is the relationship
between Israel and Islam. Without an understanding of what
is happening in the Islamic world in relation to Israel, it
is impossible to discuss the Middle Eastern problem ade-
quately. Without such an understanding, it is impossible to
grasp the enormous conflict which faces the Jewish people.

"The problem of the Middle East can only be properly
understood in theological terms. Today people find it difficult to believe that nations can still fight over religious
issues. But wars of religion are not confined to the Middle
Ages.

"What is the root cause of the whole problem? Why this
battle over Israel and the Jewish people?

"There are those who say it has to do with frontiers: 'If
only there were guaranteed and internationally recognized
boundaries, then there would be peace in the Middle East.'
Many people say that Israel should return to the borders she
had before the War of 1967. But enormous border disputes
were going on long before then. It is not simply a matter of
boundaries.

"Others blame the conflict between Zionism and the
PLO: It is said that if both these organizations ceased to

exist, then there would be peace in the Middle East. But the conflict goes back much further than the existence of either Zionism or the PLO.

"Neither can this strife be attributed to economic forces. Israel is the same size as Wales, or the North Island of New Zealand, or the state of Indiana in the USA. She is smaller than Holland or the Kruger National Park in South Africa. It is incredible that the nations round about Israel, with their vast territories, should want to take over this little strip of land, which is like a postage stamp in comparison with the Arab countries.

"Israel has no great rivers. Compared with the Nile, the Tigris, and the Euphrates, the Jordan is merely a stream. The conflict is not about water. Furthermore, Israel has no oil or gas, and no coal, diamonds, or gold. Clearly there can be no economic cause for the Middle Eastern problem. There must be a much deeper reason.

"As we have already seen, the conflict is one of *religion*. The battle is not between the might of Islam and the Jew, nor even between Islam and Zionism. Israel lies at the very heart of a violent confrontation between the spiritual powers of Islam and the Word of God (Daniel 10:13; Ephesians 6:12).

"Islam is supremely confident. It teaches that it has the final revelation of the Word of God and that it represents the fulfillment of the work of God among the nations of the world. Judaism and Christianity have their triumphal elements too. Daniel writes of *'one like the Son of Man'* being presented before *'the ancient of Days'* and being given *'dominion and glory and a kingdom, that all peoples, nations, and languages should serve Him'* (Daniel 7:13,14). Isaiah writes of the peoples and the nations who will go up to the mountain of the Lord, to the house of the God of Jacob:

> *For out of Zion shall go forth the law, and the word of the* Lord *from Jerusalem* (Isaiah 2:3b).

"These words have a ring of conviction and of triumph about them. The New Testament says, in Philippians 2:10,11:

> *... that at the name of Jesus every knee should bow, of those in heaven, and of those on earth, and of those under the earth, and that every tongue should confess that Jesus Christ is Lord, to the glory of God the Father.*

"It is this, the very essence of the faith of both the Old and New Testaments, which is rejected by Islam. For, according to Islam, these expressions of faith merely represent a passing phase. Allah has moved on and Islam is now the final phase of his work, the fulfillment of his word, and his final word to mankind. It is thus that Muhammad proclaims that Islam has replaced both Judaism and Christianity."[2]

While Judaism and Christianity each have a triumphal element, each strives to attain its respective aims in its own way. Although Judaism does not encourage proselytism, conversions have taken place since Old Testament times, and they still happen today. The Jews have lost so many of their faithful people down through the ages that orthodox Jewry is now pleading for a return to the Torah (Genesis, Exodus, Leviticus, Numbers, and Deuteronomy), to the faith of the fathers, and to the traditions of Judaism. This plea to return to both faith and practice is directed primarily toward the Jewish people themselves.

Christianity, on the other hand, is known for its outreach in response to the biblical commission of Matthew 28:18-20. At the heart of this commission to proclaim the good news to the ends of the earth, is concern for the salvation of the individual—indeed, of many individuals.

Islam has little interest in the individual, for whatever happens in the life of any person is already predetermined:

> Every man's fate
> We have fastened
> On his own neck:
> On the Day of Judgment
> We shall bring out
> For him a scroll,
> Which he will see
> Spread open (Sura 17:13).

> Say: "Nothing will happen to us
> Except what Allah has decreed
> For us: He is Our Protector":
> And on Allah let the Believers
> Put their trust (Sura 9:51).

Allah has no special concern for particular people. Islam teaches that he has a completely different role: Allah is not a father to any individual; he is the leader of the community. In Islam, more importance is given to the community as an entity than to any one individual within it. And the politics of the community are far more important than any considerations of personal religion. Islam is concerned not so much with the numbers of those who accept the faith as with the size of the territory under its control.

As we have already seen the word "Islam" means "submission." To spread the faith is to spread the might of Allah. The power of Islam is the might of Allah. Allah is the leader, the ruler, the king of kings, and the chief of staff of the Islamic army. He delegates his authority to the Caliph and to the temporal leaders of the community.

Islam sees itself as the ultimate, perfect word of Allah. The spreading of this word is not to be done simply by persuading others to become Muslim; it is Allah himself who decides who is to embrace the faith. Throughout the centuries the leaders of Islam have attempted to bring people into the fold by persuasion or force, but these have never been the usual means of making new converts. The purpose has not been primarily to create individual Muslims but rather an Islamic society.

Islamic domination has never been complete. In any particular region there have always been groups of people who have not become Muslim. This is no accident, for people were often encouraged not to change their religion. Islam was so organized that it offered the possibility of "outsiders" living as non-Muslims within Islamic society. Sometimes the existence of non-Muslim groups had important economic implications. But this is not to say that non-Muslims had equal status in society, for "Islam is superior, and nothing can supersede it."

3

The Origin and Rise of Islam

//

*I*slam is the only world religion which has come into being since the birth of Christianity. It has more than a billion followers, and their number is increasing rapidly. It began in the seventh century A.D., during a time of obvious decadence within the Christian church.

In order to understand the emergence of Islam, it is important for us to know something about the development of Christianity between the times of the Acts of the Apostles and the seventh century. The early chapters of Acts are full of accounts of vibrant and dynamic new life. We are introduced to men and women filled to overflowing with the Spirit of God. We learn about the birth of the Christian community and the missionary zeal of the apostles and the other believers, which led to a rapid expansion of the church into Asia Minor, North Africa, and Europe. We read of famous names, of preachers and teachers and defenders of the faith. But already, even in those early days of miracles and of the mighty moving of the Spirit of God, there were signs of spiritual decay. In his first letter to the Corinthian believers, the apostle Paul writes uncompromisingly about the unspiritual life of their congregation.

By the sixth century the church had become a vast organization, but living faith had been largely reduced to adherence to rigid theological formulas. Christianity had lost both her spiritual power and her missionary vision. Her former high level of morality was now hardly ever heard of, something which Paul had already foreseen (Acts 20:29). This situation was an ideal breeding-ground for the birth and growth of Islam.

Very little is known of the history of the Arabs before the birth of Muhammad, except what we have in the form of poetry and legends handed down from one generation to another. The Arab people lived in tribes, often far apart from one another and without any form of central government. Some of these tribes were very powerful, and they were often at war with their neighbors. The Quraish, who were Muhammad's tribe, controlled most of the Arabs' holy shrines, of which the most important was the *Ka'aba* (Arabic *ka'bah*, "square building"), the Muslim sanctuary in Mecca. It is here that the famous Black Stone is to be found. Muslims believe that this stone fell from heaven and was given to Abraham by the angel Gabriel. Some also believe that the stone has the power to "absorb all sin into itself" when it is kissed. This same stone was worshiped as the god of the rocks (one of 365 gods) long before the birth of Muhammad.

In these early days of Islam various Jewish communities were also living in the Arab world. They had probably fled from the land of their fathers during the Roman persecutions.

The Christian communities were less numerous than those of the Jews, and there were only a few among them who had any real desire to proclaim the gospel.

The most important centers of Christianity were in Yemen in the south, Syria in the north (both now almost completely Muslim), and Hijaz. Ethiopia was also Christian. (Today, of course, it has a very large Muslim community.)

Muhammad was born in Mecca in 570 A.D. His tribe, the Quraish, claimed to be descended from Abraham through Ishmael. Many of the Quraish were traders, and with their caravans they traveled to Syria and Yemen, among other places. Muhammad's father, Abdullah, died before Muhammad was born. His mother, Amina, died when he was six years old. After her death he was cared for by his grandfather, Abdul Mutalib, who was the acknowledged leader of Mecca and the ruler of the Ka'aba. Two years later he also died, and Muhammad's uncle, Abu Talib, a poor merchant-trader, undertook his further upbringing. During his early years Muhammad used to accompany his uncle on his journeys to Syria.

When he was 25 years old Muhammad married a wealthy widow, Khadijah. She was nearly 40, and he had worked in her service as a caravan leader. She bore him two sons, who died in infancy, and four daughters, one of whom was Fatima, who later married the Caliph Ali.

Little is known of the first 15 years of his marriage, but because of it Muhammad became an important man. Since his wife was a woman of some means, he had ample time to retreat to the mountains around Mecca for uninterrupted religious meditation.

It is said that Muhammad received his first revelation in his fortieth year, on the slopes of Mount Hira, just outside Mecca. It was during one of his periods of meditation that he was visited by a spiritual being who is supposed to have said to him three times, "Read!" Since Muhammad could neither read nor write, he took this to mean "Recite!" The content of this first revelation is probably Sura 96:1-5 ("Sura" means a section of the Qur'an):

> Proclaim! (or Read)
> In the name of thy
> Lord and Cherisher, Who created—
> Created man, out of

> A (mere) clot
> Of congealed blood:
> Proclaim! And thy Lord
> Is Most Bountiful—
> He Who Taught
> (The use of) the Pen,—
> Taught man that
> Which he knew not.

Muhammad speaks with respect of Adam and Noah, and of Abraham, Moses, and Jesus, recognizing them as prophets who preceded him. But he now sees himself as the last of them, the "seal of the prophets" (Sura 33:40), and because of this his own revelations must from henceforth be considered as having equal weight with those of all the prophets before him.

> From that time on, Muhammad tells of countless revelations. Some came directly from Allah (*tanzil*, "sent down"), while others, according to Muhammad, were given to him by the archangel Gabriel.[3]

When his revelations first began, Muhammad was terrified and wondered whether he was being attacked by evil spirits.

> This revelation was a very emotional experience for Muhammad and, trembling, he sought comfort from his wife Khadija. She played an important part in establishing him in his role as a prophet. When, for a long period of time, he received no further revelations, he reached a point of real crisis and shock, and for a time he seriously contemplated suicide.[4]

Particularly in the initial phase of his public appearance as a prophet, Muhammad is frightened and anxious about himself and he thinks he is possessed. He doubts the source of the mysterious voice which he hears and he wonders if it is a true message from God.[5]

The teachings and the morality which Muhammad began to preach as a result of his revelations, and which became the basis for the whole system which he founded, make one suspect that he was indeed controlled by supernatural powers. But his wife believed in him, and she encouraged and supported him by using her personal wealth to help the promotion of his teachings.

———————

Through his contacts with Jews and Christians in Hijaz, and during his commercial journeys, Muhammad had acquired some knowledge of Jewish and Christian beliefs. He later introduced into Islam some of the words and ceremonies he had gleaned from Judaism and Christianity (for example, fasting and formal liturgical prayers). That he knew something of these two faiths is evident from the Qur'an, but it is clear that he never had any real knowledge of the Bible.

The way he tries to retell biblical stories is enormously confusing. In one passage of the Qur'an, Mary the mother of Jesus is clearly being referred to but the impression given is that this same Mary has been confused with Miriam, the sister of Aaron and Moses. Here are some further illustrations of this kind of confusion:

Pharaoh said: "O Haman!
Build me a lofty palace,
That I may attain

The ways and means—
The ways and means
Of (reaching) the heavens,
And that I may mount up
To the Allah of Moses;
But as far as I am concerned,
I think (Moses) is a liar!"
(Sura 40:36,37).

(Haman would here appear to be Pharaoh's servant.)

Has the story of
The Disputants reached thee?
Behold, they climbed over
The Wall of the private chamber;*
When they entered
The presence of David,
And he was terrified
Of them, they said:
"Fear not: we are two
Disputants, one of whom
Has wronged the other:
Decide now between us
With truth, and treat us not
With injustice, but guide us
To the even Path. . . .
"This man is my brother;
He has nine and ninety
Ewes, and I have (but) one:
Yet he says, 'Commit her
To my care and is (moreover)
Harsh to me in speech.' "
(David) said: "He has

---

* of King David.

Undoubtedly wronged thee
In demanding thy (single) ewe
To be added to his (flock of)
Ewes: truly many
Are the Partners (in business)
Who wrong each other:
Not so do those who believe
And work deeds of righteousness,
And how few are they?"...
And David gathered that We
Had tried him: He asked
Forgiveness of his Lord,
Fell down, bowing
(In prostration), and turned
(To Allah in repentance).
So We forgave him
This (lapse): he enjoyed,
Indeed, a Near Approach to Us,
And a beautiful Place
Of (final) Return (Sura 38:21-25).

Here Nathan's sentence on David, Solomon's administration of justice, and the lost sheep of Luke 15 are thoroughly mixed up to form the content of these quranic verses.

It is clear that Muhammad developed a growing aversion to what he regarded as the pagan practices of his own people, who worshiped many gods. It is very likely that during this period of his life Muhammad was seeking for something which could truly satisfy the hunger in his heart. In his quest he encountered the Jews, and from them he heard truths from the Torah and teachings from Jewish tradition. However, he and his revelations were rejected by the Jews.

Muhammad also found little encouragement from the Christian church. As we have already seen, Christendom was in a deplorable state. (Christendom in this context, refers to the institution later known as Roman Catholicism which was already exerting its stranglehold on the true faith.) Though Muhammad picked up some fragments from the New Testament, he heard more about "stories of the saints." What appealed to him most about both Judaism and Christianity was their monotheism, but he then became very confused by the church's teaching on the Trinity.

In 451 A.D. the Council of Chalcedon had considered the question of whether the nature of Jesus on earth was human or divine. If He were God, then Mary His mother, as the bearer and mother of God, would be elevated to the level of a superhuman.

It seems that the nominal Christians of his day taught Muhammad so inaccurately about the way God had revealed Himself that he was led to understand that the "the three" were God, Jesus, and Mary. He reacted violently to this teaching: One could worship only Allah, and him alone. Muhammad speaks of this in the Qur'an:

> And behold! Allah will say:
> "O Jesus, the son of Mary!
> Didst thou say unto men,
> 'Worship me and my mother
> As gods in derogation of Allah'?"
> He will say: "Glory to Thee!
> Never could I say
> What I had no right
> (To say). Had I said
> Such a thing, Thou wouldst
> Indeed have known it.
> Thou knowest what is
> In my heart, though I

Know not what is
In Thine. For Thou
Knowest in full
All that is hidden"
(Sura 5:116).

The distorted information Muhammad received from the Christians led him to teach about one God, while rejecting the divine origin of Jesus.

With his defective knowledge of the New Testament, Muhammad returned to the Jews and fiercely denounced them for their attitude toward Jesus. Moreover, he wanted to convince them that he, Muhammad, was the Messiah, and that as such he should be recognized by them. However, the Jews totally rejected him, and from that time on a deep resentment appeared in his teachings wherever the Jews are mentioned. The Qur'an gives many examples of his feelings toward the Jews, as he curses them:

And well ye knew
Those amongst you
Who transgressed
In the matter of the Sabbath:
We said to them:
"Be ye apes,
Despised and rejected."
So We made it an example
To their own time.
And to their posterity,
And a lesson
to those who fear Allah
(Sura 2:65,66).

Say: "Shall I point out
To you something much worse
Than this, (as judged)

By the treatment it received
From Allah? Those who
Incurred the curse of Allah
And His wrath, those of whom some
He transformed into apes and swine,
Those who worshipped Evil;—
These are (many times) worse
In rank, and far more astray
From the even Path!"
(Sura 5:60).

Muhammad also claimed that he was bringing the final revelation of God to the Christians of his day. He appealed to the words of Jesus, who had promised to send the Paraclete, the One who would lead them into all truth. To this the Christians replied that the Paraclete, God's Holy Spirit, had already come ten days after Jesus' ascension into heaven (Acts 1 and 2). Therefore Muhammad, presenting himself as the paraclete some 500 years later, could not possibly be "God's final revelation." Nevertheless, in many ways Muhammad achieved a lasting effect on his audiences. Although he could neither read nor write, he was able to pass on his thoughts in beautiful Arabic, inspired as he was by a very fascinating spirit. In this way the Qur'an came into being.

The word *qur'an* means "that which must be recited." Muhammad's listeners, spellbound by his teaching, noted down every word which fell from his lips. But it was a later successor, Caliph Othman, who in 650 A.D. collected all his sayings together and gave us the book now known as the Qur'an.

When Muhammad first began to share his teachings, only a few members of his family in Medina accepted his message. The inhabitants of Mecca, which included an affluent class of Jews, resisted him for both political and commercial reasons. It was not long before Muhammad began to resort to raiding trading caravans. The caravaners were given two choices: either pay heavy taxes or convert to Islam. Though conducted on a small scale, this policy led to some great gains for Muhammad, and these were seen as divine affirmation of his mission.

> History relates that Muhammad now determined to propagate his religion by force, if no other means were effective.
> Angry with the Jews in Medina who had turned against him, he savagely turned on them. In one day his men beheaded between six and nine hundred Jewish men. Their wives and children were sold as slaves, and their property was confiscated by the Muslims.
> Muhammad then began to subdue the tribes around Mecca. In 628 A.D. he made a treaty with the people of Mecca and signed a ten-year truce which would permit him and his followers to make the pilgrimage there. The following year Muhammad entered Mecca as a pilgrim, with about two thousand followers.[6]

The spread of Islam was phenomenal. In the whole world, no previous ideology has increased so rapidly. Within a single century Islam had conquered Saudi Arabia, the entire Middle East, Central Asia, and large parts of India. It raged as a storm through Egypt, which at that time was an important center of Christianity, and the Christian communities were subjected to Islamic rule.

Islam spread through the whole of North Africa, including all the great centers of Christianity along the coast, particularly in the region of modern Tunisia. Its advance gradually extinguished the church in North Africa. It is hard to believe that, before the advent of Islam, flourishing Christian communities abounded in this part of the world.

> The above-mentioned countries [except North Africa] were under Byzantine domination. Byzantium was the Eastern Roman Empire, whose capital was Constantinople. Though nominally Christian, they neither demonstrated their faith nor offered any resistance to the Muslim forces; indeed, they seemed to welcome the invaders. The Byzantine Church was very largely a corrupt secular power exhibiting no spiritual life. As a result, the Muslims were regarded as liberators rather than invaders. This was particularly so in Egypt, where the small Christian community had been resisting the Byzantine Church. They welcomed the Islamic forces, and between 638 and 640 A.D. the whole of the Nile Delta was taken by only ten thousand men.[7]

The Islamic hordes crossed the Strait of Gibraltar and within a few years conquered almost three-quarters of Spain and Portugal. Furthermore, by the seventh century Islam had within its grasp the possibility of subduing the whole of France. It already had a third of the country within its power when, in 732 A.D., it was suddenly halted in its tracks at the battle of Poitiers, barely 125 miles from Paris. The French army was led by Charles Martel, and it won the battle even though it was overwhelmingly outnumbered by the Muslim forces. In spite of their defeat (they were forced to retreat to Spain), the Islamic army was flushed with victory because, until this setback, they had achieved success after success. In Spain their influence lived on for a few more centuries, until they were slowly driven back to North Africa.

Had Islam won the battle of Poitiers, Paris would have fallen, and with her all the areas already under the influence of Christianity, including the whole of France, the Netherlands, and a part of Germany. Within a short time Islamic soldiers could have crossed to England. Historians agree that Islam had victory within its grasp at Poitiers, but it suffered a wholly unexpected defeat. It was that defeat which, for the time being, put a halt to its advance into Europe.

A second powerful attempt to subjugate all of Europe was made during the seventeenth century by the Turks of the advancing Ottoman Empire. First Greece was conquered, then Yugoslavia and Bulgaria. Part of Romania and most of Hungary followed. By 1683 the Ottoman army had reached the gates of Vienna. In the battle that followed it was as if the whole fate of Christian Europe was hanging by a thread. Vienna was saved by a miracle. The city's 20,000 defenders had to resist a Muslim army of 300,000 men. Once again Islam was defeated. Without its defeat, the entire heartland of Europe would have been open to domination by the Ottoman Empire. It was only in the seventeenth century that the military adventures of Islam came to an end.

Following the failure of its second attempt to take over Europe, Islam fell into a state of depression and stagnation. Its culture and civilization had suffered a severe reversal, and it went into a sharp decline.

4

Muhammad
and the Bible

//

*A*ccording to Islam there are
three "holy books": the Law
(*tawrat*) and the Psalms (*zabur*), the New Testament (*injil*),
and the Qur'an. For Muhammad the Qur'an was the revelation of final and absolute truth. It replaced the Old and New
Testaments and corrected the errors which had supposedly
crept into the revelation that Allah had previously given to
the Jews and the Christians.

In asserting that the Jews had twisted the words of God,
Muhammad was specifically referring to the promises given
to Abraham and recorded in the Scriptures. These include
the promises which God has fulfilled through the line of
Isaac, Jacob, Judah, and Israel, as well as those which await
fulfillment. But, according to Muhammad, the major promises from Allah were not given to *Isaac* but to *Ishmael*.

When we consider Muhammad's attitude to the Jews, it is
important to realize that we are not merely dealing with a
casual discussion about human relationships. The issue here
is the entire revelation of the God of Israel and the existence
of the Jewish people as the people of God, and therefore the
whole truth of God's Word.

———————

At first Muhammad's attitude toward the Jews was very
favorable. Did they not share the belief that there is one
God, that He is One? And Muhammad adopted Yom Kippur

(the Day of Atonement) as a day to be observed. He also chose Jerusalem as the city toward which prayer was to be directed. However, he replaced the Sabbath (Saturday) with Friday, not as a day of rest but rather as a day of special prayer, when normal work is carried on.

This change of the Sabbath was of far more significance than the mere alteration of a weekday. In the Bible, and in Judaism to this day, observance of the Sabbath is one of the most revered of God's commandments. For orthodox Jews every day of the week is centered around the Sabbath: *"Remember the Sabbath day, to keep it holy."* Wednesday, Thursday, and Friday are the days before the Sabbath, and Sunday, Monday, and Tuesday are the days which follow. You live looking forward to the Sabbath, and you savor it afterward.

There is a dialogue in Jewish tradition which represents a conversation between God and Israel:

> God: If you accept my Torah and respect my laws, I shall give you my most precious possession to keep forever.
>
> Israel: What is the most precious thing You will give us if we obey Your Torah?
>
> God: The world to come.
>
> Israel: Then we should have a foretaste of that world to come.
>
> God: The Sabbath will give you a foretaste. Remember the Sabbath day and keep it holy.

On the Sabbath, Israel remembers the day on which God rested. Muhammad changed both the day and its meaning. That he did this quite deliberately is clear from the Qur'an:

We created the heavens
And the earth and all
Between them in Six Days,
Nor did any sense
Of weariness touch Us
(Sura 50:38).

This is obvious rebellion against one of God's most holy ordinances, which was given to the Jewish people after their deliverance from Egypt. In every celebration of Shabbat (the Sabbath) Israel relives not only her deliverance from bondage, but also her receiving of the Law.

We have seen that Muhammad turned against the Jews when they refused to recognize him as the final prophet of God. Increasingly he referred to them as merely "one of the nations." There is a remarkable parallel here with the official doctrine of the institutional church. This teaching was already embodied in Roman Catholicism, and it holds that, while Judaism may be acceptable as a religion for the individual Jew, neither Roman Catholicism nor traditional Protestant Christianity consider the return of the Jews (and their restoration as God's people in His land, the land of Israel—Isaiah 14:1a) to be the fulfillment of the prophetic Scriptures, either at the present time or in the future.

Muhammad looked on his followers as the new people of God, thus rejecting the setting apart of Israel as God's chosen people. He needed the Jews at first because, as "People of the Book," they testified to one God. But in his own versions of the biblical stories he maintained that the real truth had now been revealed to him. With this assertion, he labeled both the Old and New Testaments as counterfeit. Kohlbrugge describes this development as follows:

To this is added the totally divergent presentation of revelation in the Qur'an. At the end of the story of Joseph, we read in the Qur'an:

> Such is one of the stories
> Of what happened unseen,
> Which We reveal by inspiration
> Unto thee [Muhammad]: nor was thou
>   (present)
> With them when they [Joseph's brothers]
> Concerted their plans together
> In the process of weaving their plots
> (Sura 12:102).

The story of Noah is concluded with almost the same words, while in the story of Mary they come at the beginning. Something important is being said, which needs repeating time and again. The prophet was not present at a particular event, yet he knows something of which he could have no knowledge at all, so it becomes revelation. And that Muhammad may surely know, it is said, "Remain waiting patiently; for the outcome is for the benefit of those who fear."

These words are intended to encourage Muhammad and give him patience, and they are meant to put to shame those who whisper that he got his knowledge from elsewhere. Even though there is a story about Joseph in the Old Testament, and the Jews of Medina would have known it well, the version in the Qur'an is so new that it must be called new revelation.

Each Bible story is given a new dimension, tailor-made to the new Arabic revelation. Time and again we are told it is an Arabic Qur'an. It is a portion from Allah's book, received from heaven by the prophet, as Moses received the *tawrat* and Jesus the *injil* (Gospels).

The history of salvation has been given a new direction. No longer does Allah descend to reveal himself, but he sends down his messages and the one message remains constant: there is only one God. Thus Muhammad is relieved of the duty of being in contact with the Jews in his area and of having to acquaint himself with what was actually written in their Scriptures. Allah now reveals his story in a new, up-to-date version.[8]

In this way Muhammad can now very conveniently propose that each revelation annuls the previous one. As J. Verkuyl says:

The contents of the original *kitab* (book) have been corrupted (*muharraf*). Most Muslims believe that the Bible texts written in Hebrew and Greek, including all modern vernacular translations, have been falsified.

Muslims say that the Bible has a number of reliable sections, for example, those which deal with the oneness of God, punishment and reward, and some of the prophets. But they also argue that large parts of the Bible are unreliable and the result of counterfeit and corruption. For example, the counterfeit texts are those dealing with the divine sonship of Jesus, his cross and resurrection, and those concerning the Trinity. And many Muslim publications state that current versions of the Bible leave out whole sections, including any testimony to the coming of the *nabi* (prophet) Muhammad.

According to Muslims only one *injil* (gospel) was given to *nabi 'Isa* (Jesus) *Ruh Allah* (God's Spirit)" [referring to Jesus], and this original gospel has been hidden by certain Christians. It is alleged that this missing gospel has been replaced by four others whose aim is to raise Jesus above Muhammad.

According to Muslim tradition (*hadith*), the same corruptions have been made to other books of the Bible, so there is considerable resistance among Muslims to reading the Judeo-Christian Scriptures. We also need to remember that there is still further prejudice to contend with because Muslims believe that the whole authority of the Bible has been taken away and replaced (*mansukh*) by the Qur'an.

Islam also holds that the authority of any God-given *kitab* (book) is canceled by the next *kitab*. For example, the authority of the *tawrat* (the law) was canceled by the *zabur* (the psalms) which followed after. In the same way, the authority of the *kitab zabur* is replaced by the *injil* (the New Testament), which was revealed to *nabi 'Isa* (Jesus). Finally, the authority of the whole Bible was superseded by that of the Qur'an.

The Qur'an contains all necessary wisdom, guidance and truth, and so, according to this line of reasoning, the Bible has been surpassed and obliterated and it has become obsolete (*mansukh*).[9]

Verkuyl tells us that this belief is not asserted so strongly in the Qur'an, but Islamic tradition has given it its strength by appealing to Sura 2:106:

> None of Our revelations
> Do We abrogate
> Or cause to be forgotten
> But We substitute
> Something better or similar:
> Knowest thou not that Allah
> Hath power over all things?

Verkuyl states that this verse was not intended by Muhammad to be used against the Jewish and Christian Scriptures but rather to refer to his own earlier pronouncements. But this is far from evident in Islamic practice.

Muhammad's approach to the Bible can be looked at in various ways. The Jews wrote both the Old and New Testaments. Theologians are not agreed as to whether Muhammad was denouncing them for falsifying the text or accusing them of wrongly interpreting the Word of God. But the Qur'an is very clear on this question:

> But because of their breach
> Of their Covenant, We
> Cursed them, and made
> Their hearts grow hard:
> They change the words
> From their (right) places
> And forget a good part
> Of the Message that was
> Sent them. . . .
> From those, too, who call
> Themselves Christians,
> We did take a Covenant,
> But they forgot a good part
> Of the Message that was
> Sent them: so We estranged
> Them, with enmity and hatred
> Between the one and the other,
> To the Day of Judgment.
> And soon will Allah show
> Them what it is
> They have done.
> O People of the Book!
> There hath come to you
> Our Apostle, revealing
> To you much that ye
> Used to hide in the Book,
> And passing over much

(That is now unnecessary):
There hath come to you
From Allah a (new) light
And a perspicuous Book . . .
(Sura 5:13-15).

Theologians are even less agreed about Muhammad's own rendering of the Bible. Wessels, who is a scholar of Islam, writes:

> It is probably too simplistic to speak either of confusion or mistakes. For example, it would seem unlikely that Muhammad ever thought that Jesus and Moses were cousins. The Qur'an appears to make links which, while they do not "tie-up" on historical grounds, are designed to suit his message. The Qur'an is not concerned about giving information; its purpose is to impart this message.[10]

Wessels believes that the Qur'an cannot be judged by whether Muhammad renders the biblical stories accurately or inaccurately. He points out that the accounts of Muhammad's own life and community are just as haphazard. His line of reasoning leads him to the following justification of Muhammad's handling of the Bible:

> This is why the style of the Qur'an can be called evocative, arousing feelings rather than giving descriptions of something or someone. Its first concern is to admonish and teach. Its contents are prescriptive, rather than descriptive or informative. It wishes to speak to its reader, and to involve him in its message. It wants to bring people out of their erring ways, make the blind

see, and give the ignorant knowledge and insight.[11]

If this seems incredible, it is equally astonishing to read
what Slomp says in his review of Wessel's book:

> I sometimes wonder how much of the Qur'an
> would remain if all the Bible stories, and the
> allusions to the Bible, were omitted. Jews and
> Christians meet so much in the Qur'an which is
> familiar from their own heritage. How could we
> handle this?[12]

But in fact what Slomp calls "... Bible stories, and ...
allusions" have very little relation to the Bible. Were we to
take Slomp's remarks seriously, we might come to the conclusion that Jews, Christians, and Muslims believe in the
same God. We shall be returning to this subject later.

————————

Muhammad's claim that the Jews falsified and wrongly
interpreted God's revelation to them needs further examina-
tion. How can anyone who lived between the sixth and
seventh centuries A.D. speak about falsifying revelations
which had been given many centuries before he ever lived
(1500 B.C. to 90 A.D.)? Where are all the original revelations which the Jews are supposed to have falsified, and
what are they? There must first be an original to falsify. In
the light of Muhammad's use of his strange ideas about the
Bible, we have to ask ourselves what his part was in the
formation of the Qur'an. The answer seems obvious.

Every part of the Qur'an which is not in agreement with
the Bible must be Muhammad's own words or the words he
received by "revelation." But he could not give a single
proof that his revelations were the truth. He could only say

that, in his opinion, the Scriptures handed down by the Jewish people were not the true revelation of God. And he made this assertion without the backing of any objective or comparative evidence.

It is at this point that both Jew and Christian can no longer carry on any discussion with Islam, because their faith is founded on the fact that the Bible is God's Word, the only true revelation of Himself.

5

The Teaching of Islam

###

*I*n the past, both Jews and Christians have written books which discuss and comment on the Scriptures. For example, the Jews had the Talmud and the Christians had the creeds and various catechisms as well as the writings of the church fathers. Within each of these traditions, parts were in harmony with the Bible while other parts blatantly contradicted it. Within a few years these writings came to be regarded as having the same authority as that of the Bible, and the combination of Bible, dogma, and tradition determined the development of both religions. The teachings derived from these sources affected much more than mere religious observance; rules and regulations were formulated for every area of personal and community life, and individual, living faith was soon hedged around by dogmatic authority. As the religious historian Cantwell Smith rightly emphasizes:

> There is a discrepancy between personal faith and the cumulative tradition in which one lives and in which one has been brought up.[13]

In this respect Islam has the same history as Judaism and Christianity. The origins of Islam lie in the Qur'an, and to it have been added a number of writings which concern the everyday affairs of Muslims and determine every aspect of their community life. In Islam too, tradition (*hadith*) and legend plays an important part.

In Judaism and Christianity the formulas, traditions, and injunctions which were accepted in addition to the Bible rapidly took on a life of their own, so much so that great numbers of people today no longer know what is actually written in the Bible. We might call these inherited additions to the Scriptures first-degree derivations. In the Qur'an, however, we are faced with Muhammad's own rendering of what he had heard of the alleged Scriptures from Jews and Christians. The result is that, in the Qur'an, the Bible is barely recognizable, and the teachings with constitute the basis of the faith of Islam may be called second-degree derivations.

Sometimes statements in the Qur'an or in Islamic teaching bear an apparent resemblance to some biblical texts in their phrasing and content, but this resemblance is in fact only superficial. Upon looking closely at any apparent similarities, it soon becomes clear that stories and events which seem to be based on the Bible have been distorted and changed so as to have a completely different meaning.

Elements of Islamic Teaching

1. Islam is monotheistic. Muhammad emphatically rejected every religion which recognized more than one god. In his confrontation with biblical believers he extended his views on monotheism to Christian teaching concerning the Trinity.* The decisive, all-determining creedal statement of Islam is: "Allah is greater. . . . There is no other God than Allah."

---

* It is perhaps understandable that Muhammad became confused. Sometimes Christian teaching tends to imply that we must relate to God as if He were three separate "Gods." But God, who is One, has revealed Himself to us in the Scriptures as Father, as Son, and as Holy Spirit.

Allah forgiveth not
That partners should be set up
With Him; but He forgiveth
Anything else, to whom
He pleaseth; to set up
Partners with Allah
Is to devise a sin
Most heinous indeed
(Sura 4:48).

Verkuyl writes:

> Whoever learns to know Islam and the Muslims notices that two pronouncements are central in the Muslim vision of God (Allah). Countless times we hear in the prayers the call *allahu akbar*, which means "God (Allah) is greater." And many times a day, from the minarets and in the *salat* (the prayer), the Muslim creed (*shahada*) is heard: *la ilaha illa Allah wa Muhammad rasulu Allah*, "There is no God besides Allah, and Muhammad is His prophet (or envoy)."[14]

> Allah is He, than Whom
> There is no other god...
> (Sura 59:22).

> Say: He is Allah,
> The One and Only;
> Allah, the Eternal, Absolute;
> He begetteth not,
> Nor is He begotten;
> And there is none
> Like unto Him (Sura 112:1-4).

In his book *The Challenge of Islam*, Dr. G. Bergmann

quotes the Islamic theologian Ibn Abi Zayd Qarawan on the subject of Allah:

> The faith, which is in the heart and confessed by the mouth, says that Allah is the only God, there is no other. No one is as He is. None is like unto Him.[15]

However much these statements seem to resemble passages from the Holy Scriptures, their contents are in fact not the same. Later in this book we shall be examining the meaning of the name of the Lord. For the present it is enough to say that the above-mentioned confessions of Islamic faith mean no more than "There is no other God than God" or "Allah is Allah."

In the Old Testament we read:

> *...I am the LORD, and there is no other* (Isaiah 45:18b).

and again:

> *And there is no other God besides Me* (Isaiah 45:21b).

But this verse continues even more specifically:

> *... a just God and a Savior; there is none besides Me.*

In the New Testament we read:

> *... if you confess with your mouth the Lord Jesus and believe in your heart that God has raised Him from the dead, you will be saved* (Romans 10:9).

These verses bring us to the heart of the matter: our confession of faith in the God who speaks to us promises us His salvation, and fulfills His promise. He has revealed Himself in His Word and in His Son. We therefore need to compare various aspects of the God of the Bible with Allah.

2. Islam maintains that Allah, in the depths of his being, is unknowable and inaccessible:

> He (alone) knows the Unseen,
> Nor does He make any one
> Acquainted with His Mysteries,—
> Except an apostle
> Whom He has chosen...
> (Sura 72:26,27).

Verkuyl writes:

> In his deepest being God (Allah) is and remains hidden and unknowable. He does not coincide with his attributes. The knowledge of God's (Allah's) attributes does not make it possible for men to know anything of his purpose and will for men.[16]

Budd says:

> He does not exist in anything, nor does anything exist in him.[17]

Thus, Allah hides himself from all description.

————————

One of the names given to Allah is "the Merciful Compassionate One." But this designation does not lead us to the heart of Allah. Allah as *deus revelatus* (the revealed God) shows only his outer shell. In reality he is *deus absconditus* (the hidden God). The Bible speaks of the mystery of God and reminds us that, while no man has seen Him, He has revealed His being and His very nature to us.

This is in complete contrast to Allah, who shies away even from the possibility of being described. On what then does Muhammad base his image of Allah, since the 99 names given to him by Islam are merely attributes and titles? In the Bible the name of God represents His whole being, whereas Islam claims that there is no necessary connection between Allah's being and his attributes. From this we can only conclude that either Allah does reveal himself and that Muhammad is mistaken when he says that Allah will not even allow himself to be described, or else that the attributes which Muhammad ascribes to Allah stem from his own imagination.

Can we know God? Is there a purpose behind all that He does? The answer must be "yes." In His revelation of Himself and in His relationship to mankind, the God of the Bible is wholly different from Allah. God says what He does and does what He says:

> *Surely the Lord GOD does nothing, unless He reveals His secret to His servants the prophets* (Amos 3:7).

> *The secret of the LORD is with those who fear Him, and He will show them His covenant* (Psalm 25:14).

But God has no need to justify Himself. He is sovereign, which is why it is entirely up to Him to choose how He reveals Himself, whether by act or by His Word. But whatever way He chooses, He does not remain the remote and unknown One:

God, who at various times and in different ways
spoke in time past to the fathers by the prophets,
has in these last days spoken to us by His Son . . .
(Hebrews 1:1,2a).

God created man in His own image and after His own likeness. He made it possible for us to find Him. He has revealed Himself through His Word, and by His mighty acts and miracles.

3. Allah is an absolute, autocratic ruler. He is exalted above men and has total, unlimited power. He does not have to take anyone into account and can do whatever he wishes:

> Knowest thou not
> That to Allah (alone)
> Belongeth the dominion
> Of the heavens and the earth?
> He punisheth whom He pleaseth,
> And He forgiveth whom He pleaseth:
> And Allah hath power over all things
> (Sura 5:40).

> . . . Thou givest sustenance
> To whom Thou pleasest
> Without measure
> (Sura 3:27).

We have already looked at the oneness of Allah. Although Muhammad emphatically preached this oneness, many of the statements in the Qur'an, where Allah is said to be speaking, are in the form "we" and "us." Is this the royal "we"? Or do these words stand for Allah and Muhammad? This would often seem to be so in the Qur'an, especially when Muhammad makes Allah the mouthpiece for his own feelings and ideas. Also, Islamic tradition seems to suggest that Muhammad saw himself as some kind of mediator between man and Allah. This point will be discussed later.

Apart from Genesis 1:26 (*"Let Us make man in Our image"*) and Genesis 11:7 (*"Come, let Us go down and there confuse their language"*), the first-person plural is rarely used in the Bible with reference to God. The Lord gives expression to His highest majesty and authority in the precise yet simple words *"I, the LORD, your God."* Muhammad dared not go this far, or else he would have been presenting himself as God.

The biblical prophets are the only mouthpiece of the God who declares, *"Thus says the LORD, the God of Israel,"* or *"Thus speaks the LORD of hosts."* The Scriptures declare, *"The word of the LORD came to the prophet..."* and then God speaks, *"I, the LORD...."* He whose throne is far above the clouds, who resides in the far north, lovingly says:

> *Come now, and let us reason together...* (Isaiah 1:18).

The Lord gives His people a voice in their cause:

> *... shall I hide from Abraham what I am doing?* (Genesis 18:17).

> *O my people, what have I done to you? In what have I wearied you? Answer me! For I brought you up from the land of Egypt, and redeemed you from the house of bondage* (Micah 6:3,4 RSVB).

These are not the words of a God who is an autocratic ruler. God has made promises and He has committed Himself to them in His covenants with man. Ultimately God gave His Son. When someone gives his only son, he gives himself. Through the reconciling sacrifice of His Son Jesus, God made Himself totally vulnerable. He put into the hands of man the possibility of complete forgiveness for every person, for all time and in every place. God has given man the freedom to accept or reject His offer, but He on His part remains eternally committed to it.

4. Allah is called "the Merciful Compassionate One." The Qur'an says:

> For His Mercy He specially
> Chooseth Whom He pleaseth;
> For Allah is the Lord
> Of bounties unbounded
> (Sura 3:74).

> It is not required
> Of thee (O Apostle),
> To set them on the right path,
> But Allah sets on the right path
> Whom He pleaseth (Sura 2:272).

> Whom Allah leaves straying,—
> Never wilt thou find
> For him the Way
> (Sura 4:143).

> It is your Lord
> That knoweth you best:
> If He pleases, He granteth
> You mercy, Or if He pleases,
> Punishment . . .
> (Sura 17:54).

But again and again the Scriptures tell us that God's heart goes out to the lost:

> *God does not take away life; instead, he devises ways so that a banished person may not remain estranged from him* (2 Samuel 14:14b NIV).

> *All we like sheep have gone astray; we have*
> *turned, every one, to his own way; and the LORD*
> *has laid on Him the iniquity of us all* (Isaiah 53:6).

> *The Son of Man has come to seek and to save that*
> *which was lost* (Luke 19:10).

And what of the Good Shepherd, who leaves his 99 sheep to go and look for the one that is lost? Verkuyl writes:

> When a Muslim says that God (Allah) is al-
> mighty, it means that God (Allah) is able to do
> whatever pleases him. He can forgive, but he can
> also not forgive. And when they confess that God
> (Allah) is "rahman" and "rahim," the merciful
> compassionate one, it means that he can grant
> forgiveness to whomever he is pleased with, but
> also that he can refuse forgiveness.[18]

How utterly different is the merciful God of the Bible, the God of Israel! He does not capriciously withhold or bestow His forgiveness whenever He pleases. On the contrary, God is well-pleased with His Son (Mark 1:11), and because of His Son He is pleased with all those who have made themselves one with Him. God gave Him to us in our weakness and He

> . . . *demonstrates His own love toward us, in that*
> *while we were still sinners, Christ died for us* (Ro-
> mans 5:8).

"All we like sheep have gone astray," but God does not abandon us. He seeks the lost so that He can impute to us, the unrighteous, the righteousness procured for us by Jesus.

> *He made Him who knew no sin to be sin for us, that*
> *we might become the righteousness of God in Him*
> (2 Corinthians 5:21).

Jesus in Islam

Is Jesus the Son of God?

It is probably because he received completely unscriptural accounts of the different ways God had revealed Himself to man that the ideas Muhammad formed about God and Jesus are so far from those of the Bible.

According to Islam, Jesus is neither God nor the Son of God (see Sura 5:116, quoted earlier). Note also this quotation:

> Allah, the Eternal, Absolute;
> He begetteth not,
> Nor is He begotten . . .
> (Sura 112:2,3).

The Qur'an denies that Jesus is the Son of God, for if He were, the implication would be that God had had children and that He must have had intercourse with a woman. For this reason God is never called "Father" in the Qur'an.

Islam does teach that Jesus was born of the virgin Mary, but only because God created him within her, as it were, "out of nothing." The Qur'an says of Mary's pregnancy and childbirth:

> So she conceived him,
> And she retired with him
> To a remote place.
> And the pains of childbirth
> Drove her to the trunk
> Of a palm-tree:
> She cried (in her anguish):
> "Ah! would that I had
> Died before this! would that
> I had been a thing

Forgotten and out of sight!"
But a voice cried to her
From beneath the (palm-tree):
"Grieve not! for thy Lord
Hath provided a rivulet
Beneath thee;
And shake towards thyself
The trunk of the palm-tree:
It will let fall
Fresh ripe dates upon thee.
So eat and drink
And cool (thine) eye.
And if thou dost see
Any man, say, 'I have
Vowed a fast to (Allah)
Most Gracious, and this day
Will I enter into no talk
With any human being' "
(Sura 19:22-26).

In spite of His supernatural conception, Jesus, according to Islam, remained merely a human being. In asserting this, Islam completely ignores the preexistence of Jesus before He became man. The Holy Scriptures, on the other hand, unequivocally affirm the eternal existence of God's only Son:

> . . . *out of you* [Bethlehem] *shall come forth to Me the One to be ruler in Israel, whose goings forth have been from of old, from everlasting* (Micah 5:2b).

> *The LORD possessed me at the beginning of His way, before His works of old. I have been established from everlasting, from the beginning, before there was ever an earth* (Proverbs 8:22,23).

*In the beginning was the Word, and the Word was
with God, and the Word was God. He was in the
beginning with God. . . . And the Word became
flesh and dwelt among us, and we beheld His
glory, the glory as of the only begotten of the
Father, full of grace and truth* (John 1:1,2,14).

According to Islam, God has no Son, yet the writer of
Proverbs asks concerning "the Most High":

*Who has ascended into heaven, or descended? . . .
What is His name, and what is His Son's name?*
(Proverbs 30:4).

And Psalm 2 speaks of the decree of the Lord:

*. . . You are My Son, today I have begotten You.
Ask of Me, and I will give You the nations for Your
inheritance, and the ends of the earth for Your
possession* (Psalm 2:7,8).

This text, and indeed this whole Psalm, refers to God's
Messiah-King, whose might and majesty far exceed that of
David. God calls Him "My Son," and the kings of the earth
are told how to meet Him, and to fall at His feet lest they
should perish before Him.

Why did Muhammad reject the fact that Jesus, God's only
Son, became man? In general, mankind simply does not
want to acknowledge who Jesus really is. People are
offended by His claim that He Himself is God. But the
Scriptures affirm that He is indeed God become man. No
one has ever seen God, but in Jesus He is made known. God
is love, and love must give itself and express itself. Jesus is
that expression of God's love. He is the Son of God, and He

> *reflects the glory of God and bears the very stamp*
> *of His nature ...* (Hebrews 1:3 RSVB).

When the Scriptures say that God's love is revealed in His Son they not only mean that Jesus showed the love of God while He was on earth, but that the whole plan of salvation which God realized through Him was also the expression of God's love.

> *In this the love of God was manifested toward us,*
> *that God has sent His only begotten Son into the*
> *world, that we might live through Him* (1 John
> 4:9).

Had Muhammad recognized Jesus as both man and God, he would have had to put himself in the position of being merely his subordinate. By exalting himself above Jesus, Muhammad declared that Jesus was not the Son of God. According to Muhammad, while Jesus is a prophet, Muhammad is *the* prophet, the seal of the prophets.

> Say: "If (Allah) Most Gracious
> Had a son, I would
> Be the first to worship"
> (Sura 43:81).

> They do blaspheme who say:
> Allah is one of three
> In a Trinity: for there is
> No god except One Allah.
> If they desist not
> From their word (of blasphemy),
> Verily a grievous penalty
> Will befall the blasphemers
> Among them.
> Why turn they not to Allah,

And seek His forgiveness?
For Allah is Oft-Forgiving,
Most Merciful.
Christ the son of Mary
Was no more than
An Apostle . . . (Sura 5:73-75).

Muhammad gives a number of biblical names and events in the Qur'an, but as we have already seen, they are extremely confused. He refers to the New Testament (*injil*) as the book which Jesus received from Allah, and he gives his own distorted renderings of it. The only names mentioned are *'Isa* (Jesus), Mary, Zechariah, and John the Baptist. The disciples are barely mentioned at all, and the Qur'an's accounts of the life of Jesus, including His words and everything He did, differ greatly from the Gospel narratives. To give but one example:

Then will Allah say:
"O Jesus the son of Mary!
Recount My favour
To thee and to thy mother.
Behold! I strengthened thee
With the holy spirit,
So that thou didst speak
To the people in childhood
And in maturity.
Behold! I taught thee
The Book and Wisdom,
The Law and the Gospel.
And behold! thou makest
Out of clay, as it were,
The figure of a bird,
By My leave,
And thou breathest into it,
And it becometh a bird

By My leave,
And thou healest those
Born blind, and the lepers
By My leave.
And behold! thou
Bringest forth the dead
By My leave.
And behold! I did
Restrain the Children of Israel
From (violence to) thee
When thou didst show them
The Clear Signs,
And the unbelievers among them
Said: 'This is nothing
But evident magic.'
"And behold! I inspired
The Disciples to have faith
In Me and Mine Apostle:
They said, 'We have faith,
And do thou bear witness
That we bow to Allah
As Muslims' " (Sura 5:110, 111).

Did Jesus Die?

The Qur'an asserts that Jesus never died. According to
Muhammad, Allah has no need for the atoning, sacrificial
death of Jesus. Muhammad even contests the historical fact
of the crucifixion: Jesus was rejected by the Jewish leaders,
but Allah did not allow Him to die on a cross. Instead, Allah
removed Him and took Him alive into heaven, while a
substitute died in His place. The Qur'an says:

... they [the Jews] said (in boast),
"We killed Christ Jesus

The son of Mary,
The Apostle of Allah";—
But they killed him not,
Nor crucified him,
But so it was made
To appear to them,
And those who differ
Therein are full of doubts,
With no (certain) knowledge,
But only conjecture to follow,
For of a surety
They killed him not...
(Sura 4:157).

If Jesus had not died, He could never have risen again on the third day. In denying the crucifixion, Muhammad rejects the work of redemption which Jesus wrought for the salvation of the world. But this was the very purpose for which God became man and lived in the world! The sacrifice which Jesus Himself made, and His resurrection which followed, are together the key to our salvation.

There were several occasions when Jesus announced His death and resurrection:

> *Then He took the twelve aside and said to them, "Behold, we are going up to Jerusalem, and all things that are written by the prophets concerning the Son of Man will be accomplished. For He will be delivered to the Gentiles and will be mocked and insulted and spit upon. And they will scourge Him and put Him to death. And the third day He will rise again"* (Luke 18:31-33).

> *... the Son of Man did not come to be served, but to serve, and to give His life a ransom for many* (Matthew 20:28).

When Muhammad speaks against the atoning sacrifice of Jesus, he asserts that God needs no mediator. For Allah, the cross is not only useless but an attack on his sovereignty. Muhammad rejects the consequences of Jesus's death and resurrection. If they never happened, then there can be no new birth. No one could be born again through the resurrection of Jesus had He not been raised from the dead.

As the apostle Paul wrote:

> *If Christ is not risen, then our preaching is vain and your faith is also vain* (1 Corinthians 15:14).

If these truths are to be rejected, then passages of Scripture such as this one must also be rejected:

> *. . . He also presented Himself alive after His suffering by many infallible proofs, being seen by them during forty days and speaking of the things pertaining to the kingdom of God* (Acts 1:3).

See also Luke 24 and 1 Corinthians 15.

It is interesting to note that neither the book of Acts nor the letters of Paul, Peter, James, or John are mentioned in the Qur'an.

Jesus: Masih or Messiah?

The idea of a Mahdi ("rightly guided one") is very much alive in Islam, and Muslims look forward to the appearance of one who will bring in the reign of Allah over the whole world in the end times. But the term "Mahdi" is not used in the Qur'an to refer to Jesus, for He is only considered to be one of the prophets. The term *al masih* is usually linked to the name *'Isa* (Jesus), but it does not carry the same significance as the word *Messiah* (the Anointed One) in the Bible. (According to Verkuyl, *masih* is used to describe someone who travels about, so that Jesus is seen primarily as a servant who spread the Word of God.)[19] The Qur'an depicts Him as a mere apostle of Allah, and denies absolutely that He could be the Son of God:

> O People of the Book!
> Commit no excesses
> In your religion: nor say
> Of Allah aught but truth.
> Christ Jesus the son of Mary
> Was (no more than)
> An apostle of Allah,
> And His Word,
> Which He bestowed on Mary,
> And a Spirit proceeding
> From Him: so believe
> In Allah and His apostles.
> Say not "Trinity": desist:
> It will be better for you:
> For Allah is one Allah:
> Glory be to Him:
> (For Exalted is He) above
> Having a son. To Him
> Belong all things in the heavens
> And on earth. And enough
> Is Allah as a Disposer of affairs.
> Christ disdaineth not
> To serve and worship Allah,
> Nor do the angels, those
> Nearest (to Allah) . . .
> (Sura 4:171,172).

In the Bible the whole concept of Jesus being the Messiah, the Christ, has a far deeper meaning: Jesus is the Lord's Anointed One, and this is directly related to His kingship. He is King, and He will be King.

> *We give You thanks, O Lord God Almighty, the One who is and who was and who is to come, because You have taken Your great power and reigned* (Revelation 11:17).

> *I have set my King on Zion, my holy hill* (Psalm 2:6 RSVB).

It is written of this Anointed One:

> *. . . therefore God, Your God, has anointed You with the oil of gladness more than Your companions* (Hebrews 1:9).

> *For the Lord God Omnipotent reigns!* (Revelation 19:6).

Islam and the Holy Spirit

Jesus promised His disciples that after Him the *paracletos* would come. The Greek word means "the One who comes alongside to help us." He is also called the Holy Spirit, and Jesus said of Him:

> *. . . He will teach you all things, and bring to your remembrance all things that I said to you* (John 14:26).

Muhammad claimed that when Jesus said this, He was referring to Muhammad! Islamic scholars teach that the word used in the New Testament is not *paracletos* but *periklitos*. This is translated into Arabic as *ahmed*, a word which gives the idea of "one who praises." Its root letters are to be found in the name Mu-ham-mad. In effect, Muhammad claimed to be the *paracletos*, in that he considered himself to be the prophet of God's highest and final revelation:

And remember, Jesus,
The son of Mary, said:
"O Children of Israel!
I am the apostle of Allah
(Sent) to you confirming
The Law (which came)
Before me, and giving
Glad Tidings of an Apostle
To come after me,
Whose name shall be Ahmad."
But when he came to them
With Clear Signs,
They said: "This is
Evident sorcery!"
(Sura 61:6).

The word *periklitos* is not in the Greek lexicon. It is an invented word, based on the Greek word *cleos*, which means "fame, reputation, praise or honor," and *peri*, meaning "around." We should note that in chapters 14, 15, and 16 of the Gospel of John, where Jesus speaks of the Holy Spirit, there is no mention of any of these words. The original word in these Scriptures is clearly *paracletos*, not *periklitos*, and He is the Spirit of Truth, not a human being but the same Holy Spirit whom Jesus asked the Father to send in His name (John 14:16):

> . . . *for He dwells with you and will be in you* (John 14:17).

God has indeed revealed Himself more closely. Jesus did go to heaven, but in His stead He sent His Spirit, the Holy Spirit whom He had promised to send. When we accept the atonement of Jesus for us and ask Him to come and live in our hearts, it is the Holy Spirit who comes into our lives, and that Holy Spirit is none other than God Himself. Immanuel, God with us, becomes God within us (John 14:15-23).

Islam and Muslim Life

According to Islamic teaching, the fate of man is irrevocably determined, and must be accepted with an attitude of unchangeable submission to Allah:

> Not one of the beings
> In the heavens and the earth
> But must come to (Allah)
> Most Gracious as a servant
> (Sura 19:93).

In the Bible, Abraham and Moses are called "friends of God" (Isaiah 41:8; Exodus 33:11), and Jesus says:

> *No longer do I call you servants, for a servant does not know what his master is doing; but I have called you friends, for all things that I heard from My Father I have made known to you* (John 15:15).

For the Muslim, Allah is not a God who relates to him as would a father who cares for him. There is no question of anyone having a father-child relationship with Allah. For Islam, such a relationship would reduce Allah to the level of mortal man, which would be very humiliating for him.

Because Allah is so exalted, and so great and unapproachable, he alone determines the lot of mankind. Everything which happens to the Muslim is decreed for him by Allah, and this applies to whatever he receives and to whatever is taken away from him. His fate has been written down; it is basically unchangeable.

The word *kismet* is a Turkish word derived from the Arabic *qismah*, which means "lot" (in the sense "draw a lot" in order to choose an option). It signifies fate or fortune. With its concept of *kismet* ("your lot"), Islam does not present the love of a righteous God but rather the strange, unfathomable darkness of a hidden God. For a Muslim, prayer cannot really change anything. He can only pray in accordance with *kismet*. But trusting in *kismet* is not actually trusting in a loving God, since it is merely anticipating the unavoidable. Worrying about what might happen in life is a futile exercise. The Qur'an says that he who throws himself into the "holy war" is proving by doing so that he is chosen by Allah, and he will not die one second earlier than has been previously determined.

While fate cannot be changed, it may sometimes be known beforehand. He who strictly observes the duties laid down in the Qur'an may conclude that he has been chosen by Allah to go to paradise.

The five most important obligations for the Muslim believer are:

1. The confession of his creed: "There is no other God but Allah, and Muhammad is his prophet." It is the statement of this creed which makes a man a Muslim.

2. Prayer, five times a day, in the direction of Mecca. Before each time of prayer, ritual washing is prescribed.

3. Almsgiving or *zakat*, a tax which amounts to between 2½ and 20 percent of annual income, depending on the source of wealth. It includes charity toward members of the family, neighbors, orphans, and other needy people.

4. Fasting during the month of Ramadan, which is the ninth month of the Muslim year. The fast is observed each day of that month between sunrise and sunset.

5. The pilgrimage to Mecca, the *haje* (or *hadj*), which the faithful Muslim must make at least once in his lifetime.

These five "pillars of Islam" clearly show that Islam is a religion of law. Obedience is the most outstanding feature of Muslim piety. Regarding this attitude, Muhammad Abdul Rauf, director of the Islamic Center in Washington D.C., says:

> The objective of Islam is to make the pious and obedient Muslim pursue salvation in the hereafter by realizing the goal of his human existence on earth. Man is here in order to obey Allah in his inner and outward life. The commission is divine and must be accepted as it has been given. It does not allow for any possibility of choice or alteration.[20]

When the faithful Muslim walks in the path (*sharia*) laid down by his law, he may expect the reward of Allah. Muhammad emphasizes the necessity of keeping the law in order to reach paradise:

> One Day every soul
> Will come up struggling
> For itself, and every soul
> Will be recompensed (fully)
> For all its actions, and none
> Will be unjustly dealt with
> (Sura 16:111).

> . . . no bearer
> Of burdens can bear
> The burden of another;
> That man can have nothing
> But what he strives for;
> That (the fruit) of his striving
> Will soon come in sight;
> Then will he be rewarded

With a reward complete;
That to thy Lord
Is the final Goal...
(Sura 53:38-42).

Islam is a religion of law. It neither redeems nor brings new birth. A religion based on law teaches that man is able to redeem himself. But the Scriptures say that a man cannot ransom his brother, let alone himself (see Psalm 49).

In the Scriptures, the law and the prophets bear witness to the righteousness of God, obtainable apart from the law. While God expects everyone to keep His law, His law is perfect and, because of this no one can possibly keep it fully.

The Scriptures therefore show us a different way to salvation. It is in fact the only way, and it consists in the believer identifying himself completely with Jesus Christ and His observance of the law:

> *But now the righteousness of God apart from the law is revealed, being witnessed by the Law and the Prophets, even the righteousness of God which is through faith in Jesus Christ to all and on all who believe* (Romans 3:21,22).

That God should sacrifice His only Son out of love for mankind is considered by Muslims to be not only absurd but also blasphemous. For Islam, Allah remains invisible and inscrutably remote from man, and whoever teaches that God became man in Jesus Christ is speaking heresy.

Muhammad's rejection of the atoning death of Jesus shows a complete lack of insight into the nature of sin. The fall of man and his resulting separation from God are mentioned in Islam but given a different meaning than what is described in the Bible. For Muhammad, sin meant a mere shortcoming, a proof of weakness. De Kruyf writes:

If sin were only something at the surface of our life, God could have been satisfied with disregarding it altogether. But because sin has affected us in our inmost being, Jesus had to identify Himself completely with us in order to help us. To put it literally, He "swapped" Himself for us, taking our place. He took upon Himself not only the effect of sin in general but also the effect of sin for which we are ourselves responsible. And He did this in order to give us a life in which we might love both God and our neighbours.[21]

The Bible and the Qur'an differ fundamentally on the question of sin and salvation, and regeneration by God's Spirit. So they are equally opposed in the way they tell us how we may obtain eternal life.

Islam, Judgment, and Eternity

Even for the Muslim, it is difficult to live according to Islamic law. There was a mystical movement within Islam from its earliest days, and this appeared to have a certain pseudo-Christian spirituality about it which was supposed to bring people closer to God. But the movement was only marginal, and most Muslims knew only that they had to obey the law.

Even though a Muslim may adhere strictly to his prescribed law, he can never be sure during his lifetime that he will attain paradise when he dies. Islamic tradition teaches that every Muslim will end up in paradise, but there are different views as to how this will happen. Paradise is not only a place for the righteous but also for the martyr, or *shahid*, the one who dies for the cause of Islam. The *shahid* gives his life for the cause of Allah in the holy war.

In their ideas concerning creation and the end of time, there are enormous differences between Islamic and biblical teaching. The element of planning, the development through which God takes His creation (one of the unique features of the Bible), is completely absent from the Qur'an. Neither is there any mention in the Qur'an of the significance in world history of the Jewish people in the land of Israel.

In Islam, creation is identified with the world. It does not imply a promise of revelation and salvation, as it does for the Jews and Christians. The world may have been brought into being by Allah, but, once created, there is no need for change. If any change or improvement is to come, it can only come about as a result of the extension of the kingdom of Islam over the whole world. The world stands on its own; it has been determined by a past act of creation rather than by what is yet to come. It is merely a mosaic, designed by Allah, in which there are no clear historical or geographical frames of reference.

In Islamic tradition there is mention of a great war which will take place at the end of time. This is somewhat similar to the Gog-Magog war (*Jadjudj* and *Mahjudj*), but no specific battleground is indicated. The Qur'an does touch on certain future matters such as the end of time, the second coming of Jesus, and the last judgment. The return of Jesus is considered to be a "sign of the times."

> He [Jesus] was no more than
> A servant: We granted
> Our favour to him,
> And We made him
> An example to the Children
> Of Israel.
> And (Jesus) shall be

A Sign (For the coming
Of) the Hours (of Judgment):
Therefore have no doubt
About the (Hour), but
Follow ye Me: this
Is a Straight Way
(Sura 43:59,61)

A commentary on Sura 43:61 says:

Jesus shall convert the Christians to Islam and
make it clear to them that it was wrong to honour
him as Son of God. Then the returned Jesus will
eradicate all those who do not turn to the true
faith of Islam. Only Islam will remain. There-
upon, Jesus will marry. After a time of paradise,
there will be unity between man and beast. This
time of paradise will last for either twenty-four or
forty years. Finally, Jesus will die and be buried
in Mecca next to Muhammad.[22]

The Qur'an describes paradise as a very real place, with
rivers flowing through gardens, beautiful trees, lovely
women, and flowing wine. It has everything which is cher-
ished but difficult to attain in this life.

According to dominant Islamic teaching, every Muslim
must have a little taste of hell before he goes to paradise.
This shows him something of the suffering of people in hell.
There is also the question of what happens when a Muslim
goes to paradise, thereby leaving a space in hell. Some say
that the almighty Allah can always find a Jew or a Christian
to fill the empty place! A milder version has it that hell for a
Muslim lasts for only 40 days. The Qur'an says:

Then guard yourselves against a day
When one soul shall not avail another,

Nor shall intercession be accepted for her,
Nor shall compensation be taken from her,
Nor shall anyone be helped (from outside)
(Sura 2:48).

Taking Islamic thought to its logical conclusion, it is evident that Jesus is no savior, nor advocate, nor protector. Neither is He our intercessor:

Not one of the beings
In the heavens and the earth
But must come to (Allah)
Most Gracious as a servant.
He does take an account
Of them (all), and hath
Numbered them (all) exactly.
And every one of them
Will come to Him singly
On the Day of Judgment.
On those who believe
And work deeds of righteousness,
Will (Allah) Most Gracious bestow Love
(Sura 19:93-96).

The absolute statements which Muhammad makes in the Qur'an concerning judgment have been somewhat modified by Islamic tradition to suggest that he almost has the role of a mediator. It is believed that on the day of judgment everyone will die. At the sound of the trumpet all will rise from death to appear before the judgment seat of Allah. The deeds of all mankind, both good and bad, will be weighed in the balance. Everyone will turn to the prophets, looking for them to intercede, but the prophets will refer them to Adam. He, only too aware of his own guilt, will refer everyone to Jesus, who will point them to Muhammad. Allah will then give Muhammad permission to intercede. In other words, on the day of judgment it is Muhammad who will fulfill the role of mediator.

Who Inspired Muhammad?

Earlier in this book we looked briefly at the history of Muhammad and the origins of the Qur'an, and we also touched on the importance which Muhammad gave to his teachings. According to Islam, the Qur'an supersedes every other divine manifestation:

> This will of Allah has been revealed to mankind by the prophets. The last in this line of prophets is Muhammad, peace be unto him. The Qur'an is the holy book of the Muslims and the only divine revelation which came to us unchanged.[23]

Once again we must ask ourselves this question: Is it the God of the Bible who reveals Himself in the Qur'an?

Islam recognizes more than one prophet. The most important of these are Noah, Abraham, Moses, Isaiah, John the Baptist, and Jesus. While God spoke through all these prophets, Muhammad is considered to be the last of the line and the one through whom God gave His final revelation.

Let us assume for a moment that this is true. We are then faced with the idea that God made known to Muhammad things which were completely opposed to what He revealed to other people. But it is inconceivable that God would contradict Himself.

God is supposed to have told Muhammad that He created Jesus in Mary's womb as a creature. In the Qur'an, Mary is quoted as saying to Allah:

> ... "O my Lord!
> How shall I have a son

When no man hath touched me?"
He said: "Even so:
Allah createth what He willeth:
When He hath decreed a plan,
He but saith to it 'Be,' and it is!"
(Sura 3:47).

But Jesus testified:

> *. . . before Abraham was, I AM* (John 8:58).

> *He who has seen Me has seen the Father* (John 14:9).

> *No one has ascended to heaven but He who came down from heaven, that is, the Son of Man who is in heaven . . .* (John 3:13).

> *I have come down from heaven, not to do My own will, but the will of Him who sent Me* (John 6:38).

God supposedly said to Muhammad:

Say, "Praise be to Allah
Who begets no son,
And has no partner in (His) dominion:
Nor (needs) He any
To protect Him from humiliation:
Yea, magnify Him
For His greatness and glory!"
(Sura 17:111).

Through the mouth of David, God speaks about His Messiah:

> *You are My Son, today I have begotten you* (Psalm 2:7).

Through Solomon, God says this:

Who has established all the ends of the earth? What is His name, and what is His Son's name . . ? (Proverbs 30:4b).

And in the presence of Peter, James, and John, God says:

This is My beloved Son, in whom I am well pleased. Hear Him! (Matthew 17:5).

God is supposed to have said to Muhammad that the crucifixion and sacrifice of Jesus never took place (Sura 4:157,158). But John the Baptist, the forerunner of Jesus (and one of the series of prophets recognized by Muhammad), witnessed concerning Jesus:

Behold! The Lamb of God who takes away the sin of the world! This is He of whom I said, "After me comes a Man who ranks higher than I, for He was before me" (John 1:29,30 marginal rendering).

And we have Jesus' own words:

The Son of Man did not come to be served, but to serve, and to give His life a ransom for many (Matthew 20:28).

It must already be clear to the objective reader that Muhammad is both contradicting himself and resisting the claims of Jesus. He states quite bluntly that many biblical texts were rendered incorrectly by their Jewish writers. If we assume that Muhammad was truly inspired, then we have to ask ourselves whether he had the same source of inspiration as his biblical predecessors.

In the light of all that has been discussed so far, we are unavoidably confronted by the following questions:

1. Is Muhammad truly a prophet who has spoken in the name of the God of the Bible?

2. Is Allah, whom Muhammad preaches, the same as the God of Israel who revealed Himself to Moses on Mount Sinai?

3. Is Allah the same as the God and Father of Jesus Christ?

4. Is Allah the same as the God of *chesed* and *chen*, the covenant-keeping and merciful God, and the God of love of whom the Scriptures testify?

5. Is Allah the same as the God of Abraham?

Under the inspiration of Allah, Muhammad (a zealous man) expressed himself with considerable fervor. It must now be clear that, whatever parts of the Bible he may have heard about, he mixed them with his own thoughts, desires, and experiences, and presented the resulting conglomeration as a flow of new revelation. This manner of speaking, which makes statements but then revokes and replaces them with something else, is not the way of the God the Bible. Neither is it the way of any of the biblical prophets, who spoke the words of God as a complete and consistent revelation.

God and the Word of God are one. He cannot revoke, deny, or abandon His Word:

> *For as the rain comes down*
> *And the snow from heaven,*
> *And do not return there*
> *But water the earth,*

And make it bring forth and bud,
That it may give seed to the sower
And bread to the eater,
So shall My word be that goes forth
From My mouth;
It shall not return to Me void,
But it shall accomplish what I please,
And it shall prosper
In the thing for which I sent it
(Isaiah 55:10,11).

If God were to abandon what He has said, He would be unfaithful to His own Word and would thereby deny Himself.

Islam: Revival and Revolution

//

*I*t was largely in the twentieth century, with the discovery of oil under
the desert sands and all the new opportunities this created,
that revival came to the Muslim world. The impetus for much
of this revival came from spiritual leaders like the Ayatollah
Khomeini, who pointed out that it was Allah who had now
given Muslims a new chance of winning the world for Islam.

Oil, and the enormous wealth it created, gave Islam the
power to influence the whole of the Western world. Money
was readily available, and, as one of the most convenient
agents of power, it played a crucial role in the change of the
fortunes of Islam.

While the development of economic growth is relatively
easy, changes in other areas of society are more difficult to
establish and therefore need more time to take root. Khomeini greatly strengthened the position of Islam in the
Middle East and even in Africa. With fanatical effort and
perseverance he hardened his grip on the Islamic nations.
Many Muslim and Arabic countries have now readopted,
wholly or partly, the *sharia*, an ancient system of Islamic law.

The Western world cannot remain untouched by this up-
surge of Islamic influence. Most Western, Christian-oriented
states are familiar with the concept of the separation of
church and state. Throughout the course of history the

church has attempted to take over the functions of the state, and at times the state has tried to be the church. (State churches still exist today.) While legislation in the West is still to some extent based upon Christianity, there is no Western nation where the state interferes simply because someone disobeys one of the biblical commandments. (This can happen only if a particular commandment has been written into secular legislation.)

This way of thinking is alien to most Islamic cultures. Where Allah is ruler, there can be no distinction between state and religion. Religion is the state, and together they form a single entity. According to one Islamic scholar:

> Islam not only means a religion for man's head, soul and heart; it is an all-encompassing culture, a theocentric society in which every area of life, education, economy, family, and politics relate to Allah. There is no question of separation between throne and pulpit or between politics and religion. The mosque is often the starting place for demonstration and political revolution, and the Friday sermon is not only a religious practice but it often fervently calls upon the faithful to take political action in the name of Allah.*[24]

For Islam, the idea of "mission" is not to seek to bring about the mere intellectual and religious conversion of people; instead, it is much more concerned with the territorial expansion of Allah's kingdom. The supreme way of bringing this about is the *jihad*, or holy war.* Regarding "infidels," the Qur'an says:

---

* A parallel is sometimes drawn between the "Christian" Crusades and the *jihad*. It is not correct to compare the excesses of one religion with the *formal teachings* of another. Cruelties perpetrated by the Crusaders cannot be justified by even a single scripture.

And fight them on
Until there is no more
Tumult or oppression,
And there prevail
Justice and faith in Allah;
But if they cease,
Let there be no hostility
Except to those
Who practice oppression
(Sura 2:193).

In Islam, the call to fight the holy war comes as a direct commandment from Allah. It is not some enterprise fool-ishly undertaken at the whim of the faithful. The possibility of such "holy war" is a very real threat today, and it should not be lightly dismissed. The Islamic scholar just quoted writes:

To grapple seriously with Islam, in order to gain any real understanding of it, a wholly new mind-set is required.

Islamic strategy divides the world into two areas. One is described as *dar-al-salaam*, the house of peace, and the other *dar-al-harb*, the house of war. The house of peace is only estab-lished when and where Islam has become the state religion and the *sharia*, the constitution of Islam, controls all aspects of life. Nations which refuse the demands of Allah, and which resist the establishment of Islamic rule, are called *dar-al-harb*.

This world-view is linked with the whole Is-lamic concept of God. In Islam, there is nothing outside Allah's power. He alone is all in all. What-ever is not given to him willingly must be brought into subjection to him by using other methods, such as economic pressure or the revolutionary power struggle. Islam means submission to Allah, and such submission means handing over every aspect of life to his spirit, in addition to accepting the authority of the Qur'an over all thought, behavior and morality. This way of thinking must become a reality for the whole world.[25]

The Wheel

Islam is today experiencing a revival in every aspect of its life, whether political, cultural, or social. This is no accident. The revival which started in the 1970's, in which Khomeini was partly instrumental, is connected with the Islamic understanding of the "end of the age."

Islam dates its inception from 570 A.D., so it is now at the beginning of its fifteenth century.

For centuries, the ultimate hope of the Jews has been the coming of the messianic kingdom, a kingdom which has to do with the appearance of the Messiah-King and with both the revival and renewal of Israel. Christians should realize that the Bible points in many places to God's millennial, thousand-year kingdom on earth (Isaiah 2:1-4; Revelation 20:4; etc.). Islam also thinks in terms of specific time-spans, but these are in *hundred-year* rather than *thousand-year* cycles. Behind this way of thinking lies the idea that the world, as far as time is concerned, goes through a kind of cyclical motion in which time is constantly returning to its starting-point.

According to this idea, the course of the world in history is not to be seen as one of forward movement. The idea of "progress" does not receive much attention in the political and philosophical thinking of Islam. Instead, as we shall see more fully, the course of world events is based on the idea of a wheel in motion, an idea which was very real to Muslims of the Middle Ages. While less stressed today, the concept is still a significant part of Islamic thought.

According to Islam, the path followed by mankind may be compared to that of a wheel turning on its axle. During the movement of turning there is always a point on the rim of the wheel which is at the top. This upper point may be considered as being at the best and most favorable position in the wheel's cycle. As the wheel goes on turning, the point which was on top now proceeds downward until it finally reaches the lowest point in the cycle. When this happens the low point has been reached, and this may be considered as representing the worst possible moment in time.

Until the recent Islamic revival, Islam tended to go along with the forward movement of humanity, but such movement is not considered to represent either progress or improvement but rather *deterioration*. For Islam there is only one way to bring about improvement, and that is to go backward in time.

The further back the wheel goes the better things will become because, it is argued, you will find yourself back at the top of the cycle all the sooner. A parallel may be drawn with the face of a clock in which the big hand is not allowed to go beyond the quarter-past mark.

So what is to be done when Islam suffers a military defeat or a political or economic setback? What is to be done when even Muslim believers seem to be losing their faith? Shall Islam go forward with the tide of history into an ever more modern way of life? Or shall it go backward into the past? Islam answers, "Go back!" For in turning back to the past the high point in the cycle of the wheel will be reached all the more quickly.

In Islam, the time-cycles last for a hundred years. It is at the end of such a period that Islam finds itself at its lowest ebb, and it is at these times that there is increased expectancy concerning a messiah.

At the turn of the fourteenth century the mosque in Mecca was captured by one calling himself the *mahdi* or savior. Five hundred years later, in 1900, yet another prophet, who called himself Muhammad son of Abdullah, led an uprising in the Sudan. And now, in the second half of the twentieth century, the crucial low point in the cycle has been reached again.

Because there is still no messiah in Islam, the answer must be to turn the wheel back so that its crucial point can once again be at the highest point of the cycle. No time in history can surpass that of the prophet Muhammad himself, and the message of Islam for the faithful today is this: "Let us return to the best of the past, to the word of the prophet, to the word of Allah and to the Qur'an. Let us turn back to the tradition, back to everything which is truly of Islam."

As we shall see in the next chapter, Khomeini actually began his crusade at the low point of the cycle, in the very middle of the twentieth century. His appearance on the world scene, however, indicated that a new Islamic age had begun. In this way Islam is taking her followers back into the world of the past.

Salaam, Shalom

The words "Islam" and "Muslim" are both formed from the root letters *s*, *l*, and *m*, which portray the idea of submission and surrender to God. Wessels writes:

> In this connection, it is interesting to listen to the description of Abraham in the Qur'an:
>
> > And remember Abraham
> > And Isma'il raised
> > The foundations of the House[26]

(With this prayer): "Our Lord!
Accept (this service) from us:
For Thou art the All-Hearing,
The All-Knowing.
Our Lord! make of us
Muslims, bowing to Thy (Will),
And of our progeny a people
Muslim, bowing to Thy (Will)..."
(Sura 2:127,128).[27]

Wessels continues:

This "surrender" to God is the true religion, and Abraham is the best example of it.[28]

In terms of its religious practice and community, Abraham lived before the development of modern Islam, as it is understood today. Yet the core of every religion is only "submission" to God. In this sense, Abraham can be called a Muslim. Similarly, the prophets can be called "muslim." And it could be said that the nucleus of their message is "islam."[29]

Abraham was indeed submitted and surrendered, but his submission and surrender were to the God who *does* have a Son. It was this Son's "day" that Abraham saw:

...Abraham rejoiced to see My day, and he saw it and was glad (John 8:56).

Returning now to the root letters *s*, *l*, and *m*, we find that they also stand for the concept of peace, in Arabic *salaam* and in Hebrew *shalom*. Islam teaches that between warring parties there must first be a period of *salaam*. In this context the word gives the idea of treating the other party without hostility while keeping a proper distance. After a period of such *salaam*, the *sulha* (the meeting for forgiveness and reconciliation) may take place.

Both the Old and New Testament express the concepts of *slicha* (which also expresses repentance and forgiveness, followed by reconciliation) and *shalom*, peace. But in the Bible, in contrast with the Qur'an, the order is reversed, for between God and man, and between man and man, forgiveness comes first. Only forgiveness can bring peace.

According to Islam there can only be peace when the whole world is submitted to Allah and to Islam. But according to the Bible, without the Son of God there can be neither forgiveness nor reconciliation, and therefore no peace.

7

Isaac and Ishmael

##

*F*rom its earliest days Islam has had an uneasy relationship with Jews and Christians. Their presence has been barely tolerated in Arab lands, and their daily life has usually been hedged about by limitations and restrictions. For Islam, Jews and Christians are not "unfaithful nonbelievers"; they are called the "People of the Book"—that is, people of the Bible.

Islam accepts Jews and Christians as "People of the Book" but restricts them from actively witnessing to their faith, especially to Muslims. They must remain silent in this regard and show respect to Islam and to the Qur'an.

In Genesis 16:1-12 we read how Abraham had a son, Ishmael, through his wife's maid, Hagar. According to Islamic tradition, it is the descendants of Ishmael who are in the divinely promised line. The Quraish tribe claim to be the descendants of Ishmael, and since Muhammad was from the same line, he claimed to be "the prophet of promise."

Islam accuses the Jews of unjustly claiming the divine inheritance for themselves. If this is true, then they must have done so some 2500 years before the birth of Muhammad! Of Muslims the Qur'an says:

Ye are the best
Of Peoples, evolved
For mankind,

Enjoining what is right,
Forbidding what is wrong,
And believing in Allah.
If only the People of the Book
Had faith, it were best
For them: among them
Are some who have faith,
But most of them
Are perverted transgressors
(Sura 3:110).

But in the Bible we see that Ishmael was not "the son of promise," for God said:

. . . Sarah your wife shall bear you a son, and you shall call his name Isaac; I will establish My covenant with him for an everlasting covenant, and with his descendants after him (Genesis 17:19).

My covenant I will establish with Isaac . . . (Genesis 17:21a).

. . . in Isaac your seed shall be called (Genesis 21:12b).

. . . for salvation is of the Jews (John 4:22).

Since the days of Abraham there has been conflict between the descendants of his two sons, and this has continued right up to the present day. Psalm 83 speaks of Ishmael joining with Edom to form a confederacy against the God of Israel and His people. Had Muhammad been a true prophet, he would have felt very positively toward Israel. Sadly, the contrary is true. He drove out and killed many Jews, and he even cursed them in the name of Allah:

They are (men) whom
Allah hath cursed:
And those whom Allah
Hath cursed, thou wilt find,
Have no one to help.
Have they a share
In dominion or power?
Behold, they give not a farthing
To their fellow-men!
(Sura 4:52,53).

Some of them believed
And some of them averted
Their faces from him* and enough
Is Hell for a burning fire.
Those who reject
Our Signs, We shall soon
Cast into the Fire:
As often as their skins
Are roasted through,
We shall change them
For fresh skins,
That they may taste
The Penalty . . .
(Sura 4:55,56).

The Scriptures say:

The LORD did not set His love on you nor choose you because you were more in number than any other people, for you were the least of all peoples; but because the LORD loves you, and because He would keep the oath which He swore to your fathers (Deuteronomy 7:7,8a).

---

* Muhammad.

> *I say then, has God cast away His people? Certainly not! . . . God has not cast away His people whom He foreknew* (Romans 11:1,2).

Suddenly, in 1948, not so far from Mecca, the very heart of Islam, a Jewish state emerged with its own President, parliament, government, prime minister, and army; it had everything which distinguishes a genuine national community. A new nation had been born, and this was a clear demonstration of the fulfillment of what had been written by the prophets:

> *I will bring back the captives of My people Israel; they shall build the waste cities and inhabit them. . . . I will plant them in their land, and no longer shall they be pulled up from the land I have given them, says the LORD your God* (Amos 9:14a,15).

> *Their descendants shall be known among the Gentiles, and their offspring among the people. All who see them shall acknowledge them, that they are the posterity whom the LORD has blessed* (Isaiah 61:9).

The rebirth of the Jewish state right in the midst of the Arab countries is a direct contradiction of Islamic teaching. Has not Allah finished with the Jewish people?* And if Allah has predetermined all things, how is it possible that a Jewish state should have come into existence once again? For Islam this is not only an impossibility but sheer foolishness. But this "foolishness" is the wisdom of God.

---

* Many Christians have believed this over the centuries, teaching that God has rejected the Jews and transferred the promises of the covenant to the church.

The birth and growth of the state of Israel can only be understood in the light of biblical revelation and cannot and should not be judged by secular standards. Even though Israel is still "the enemy of the gospel" for the sake of the Gentiles (Romans 11:28), the Jewish people are still being used by God. After 4000 years He is bringing them back to the land of their origin.

For Muslims the worst humiliation is that this Jewish state has Jerusalem as its capital. On July 30, 1980, the Knesset (the Israeli parliament) passed a law declaring the City of Jerusalem to be "eternal and indivisible."

Jerusalem occupies a comparatively small geographical area and, after Mecca and Medina, it is the third-most-holy place in Islam, for it is said that from here Muhammad was taken up into heaven on a white horse. (He is actually buried in Medina). And this same Jerusalem is now the capital of a Jewish state which, in Muslim eyes, should never have come into being!

The dispute over Jerusalem and over Israel's borders can never be settled by any boundary agreements or peace treaties. Jerusalem has to be the stumbling-block.

> *Behold, I will make Jerusalem a cup of drunkenness to all the surrounding peoples, when they lay siege against Judah and Jerusalem. And it shall happen in that day that I will make Jerusalem a very heavy stone for all peoples; all who would heave it away will surely be cut in pieces, though all nations of the earth are gathered against it* (Zechariah 12:2,3).

The Islamic powers will never acknowledge Jerusalem as the capital of the Jewish state. Neither will the Jewish people ever give up Jerusalem.

Within the city itself the real heart of the matter lies in a small central area known as the Temple Mount. It is because of this small area that Islam values Jerusalem so highly. It is here that God once asked Abraham to offer up his son Isaac. It is also the place where the LORD established His name forever (1 Kings 8:17,18,48b). On it there now stands the Dome of the Rock, the mosque of Omar. And on the place where Solomon's porch once stood, where the Holy Spirit was poured out on the first believers, and where they came together for prayer and teaching and to study the Word of God (John 10:23; Acts 3:1,11; 5:12), there now stands the El Aksa mosque. This must be a continuing blasphemy for the God of Israel. What was once the heart of Judaism and the center for believers in Jesus is now an Islamic sanctuary.

Among other quotations from the Qur'an, around the dome of the mosque of Omar are written the following words from Sura 4:171:

> . . . so believe
> In Allah and His apostles.
> Say not "Trinity": desist
> It will be better for you:
> For Allah is One Allah:
> Glory be to Him:
> (For exalted is He) above
> Having a son.

Also quoted are these words:

> It is not befitting
> To (the majesty of Allah)
> That He should beget
> A son. Glory be to Him!
> (Sura 19:35).

For nearly 1400 years the God of Israel has remained silent and restrained, but now in these present days the fulfillment of the biblical signs of Messiah's coming can be clearly seen (Psalm 102:16). The moment when He will intervene cannot be very far away.

> *Thus says the Lord GOD: "Surely I will take the children of Israel from among the nations, wherever they have gone, and will gather them from every side and bring them into their own land; and I will make them one nation in the land, on the mountains of Israel"* (Ezekiel 37:21,22a).

> *Then they shall dwell in the land that I have given to Jacob My servant, where your fathers dwelt; and they shall dwell there, they, their children, and their children's children, forever; and My servant David shall be their prince forever. Moreover I will make a covenant of peace with them, and it shall be an everlasting covenant with them; I will establish them and multiply them, and I will set My sanctuary in their midst forevermore. My tabernacle also shall be with them; indeed I will be their God, and they shall be My people. The nations also will know that I, the LORD, sanctify Israel, when My sanctuary is in their midst forevermore* (Ezekiel 37:25-28).

The End Times

What is the significance of Islam and Israel in the end times? In the Bible, the term "end times" refers to the period directly preceding the coming of the Messiah, the second coming of Jesus. This period will be marked by a number of signs. It is clear from the Bible that the most important of these is the return of the Jewish people to "Eretz Israel," the land of Israel.

> *You will arise and have mercy on Zion; for the time to favor her, yes, the set time has come. . . . So*

> *the nations shall fear the name of the LORD, and*
> *all the kings of the earth Your glory. For the LORD*
> *shall build up Zion; He shall appear in His glory*
> (Psalm 102:13,15,16).

> . . . *the disciples came to Him privately, saying,*
> *"Tell us, when will these things be? And what will*
> *be the sign of Your coming, and of the end of the*
> *age?" And Jesus answered and said to them . . .*
> *"Now learn this parable from the fig tree: When*
> *its branch has already become tender and puts*
> *forth leaves, you know that summer is near. So*
> *you also, when you see all these things, know that*
> *it is near, at the very doors. Assuredly, I say to*
> *you, this generation will by no means pass away*
> *till all these things are fulfilled. Heaven and earth*
> *will pass away, but My words will by no means*
> *pass away"* (Matthew 24:3,32-35).

> . . . *I saw your fathers as the firstfruits on the fig*
> *tree in its first season* (Hosea 9:10a).

The fulfillment of these Scriptures has undeniably been taking place since 1948. At the same time there is an almost palpable revolt against the whole idea that the modern nation of Israel represents such a fulfillment. There are many who deny Israel even the right to exist. They also deny her significance for the end times and do not accept the idea that she has an integral part to play in the future, and for eternity. But the establishment of the state of Israel has taken place, and Jews are pouring into their land. Events are overtaking the skeptics. There would seem to be little purpose in their continuing to deny what is really going on, but the opposition will not give up its fight that easily. This is why the Arab world is constantly preparing for an overwhelming attack on Israel. On the surface it might seem that the battle for the Middle East is all about the nation and the land of Israel, the city of Jerusalem and the Temple Mount. But it is important to look at what the prophets of Israel were constrained to say, both about their own times and what was for them the distant future.

A number of events predicted by the prophets have not yet taken place. An example of this is the Gog-Magog war described in Ezekiel 38 and 39. According to the Jewish historian Josephus, the term "Gog and Magog" refers to the descendants of the Scythians who lived in the Caucasian region of what is now the southwest of the USSR, between the Black Sea and the Caspian Sea. The term is also used to signify all those nations and forces of the world which are determined to destroy Israel and Jerusalem.

The Gog-Magog war described by Ezekiel will probably take place before the coming of the Messiah—that is, before the second coming of Jesus. It will be precipitated by the "power of the far north." It is generally accepted that this must refer to the Soviet Union.

Even before Israel became a nation, the Kremlin was taking into account the implications of the rebirth of the Jewish state, and it has been drawing up its plans for the Middle East for the past 40 years or more.[30] While the details of its policy may have been changed from time to time, its general aim remains unaltered.

The idea is for an outer ring of states to be laid down around Israel and the oil-producing countries, states which are either overtly Marxist or at least in some sympathy with the aims of the Soviet Union.

Israel is the only Middle Eastern power which, in the event of a third world war, would prove a real threat to the Soviet Union. The Soviet forces would need to be in a position to neutralize her within weeks of the outbreak of war. The only way this could be achieved would be by using the surrounding ring of nations to blockade Israel by land, sea, and air. The Soviet Union has never changed this objective. Its other aim is to cut off the industrialized nations of the West, including Japan, Australia, and New Zealand, from all sources of energy, particularly oil. The activities of the USSR over the past few decades, in both Asia and in Africa, only go to confirm the seriousness of its intentions.

In these days of *glasnost* and *perestroika* we might be tempted to ask ourselves whether the Kremlin has not given up this long-term aim. But history shows us that totalitarian systems, whether religious or secular, do not change their determination to establish a new world order.

There is no historical precedent for a war like that described in Ezekiel 38 and 39. At no time before in history has a confederacy of states suddenly invaded a small, isolated nation which has reappeared on the center of the world stage after its people, having been dispersed throughout the world for centuries, have been brought back to their own land.

In spite of the present cry for "peace among nations," the Word of God will prevail, and the events described in Ezekiel 38 and 39 will assuredly take place.

When war finally breaks out, a number of Islamic nations will join forces with the Soviet Union.

———————

In Ezekiel 38 and 39 several place-names occur which, when translated and brought up-to-date, almost certainly refer to territories north of the Black Sea and also to Eastern Turkey, Iran, Ethiopia, Libya, and Saudi Arabia.

The Soviet Union and the protagonists of the Islamic revolution will unite in a joint attack. The Kremlin will capitalize on Islam's deep desire to destroy Israel, and the armies of the Islamic revolution will gladly make use of

Soviet military might, which it will later seek to subdue under Islam. But God will cause them both to be defeated.

––––––––––

We have seen that the rebirth and development of the Jewish state is in contradiction to the Qur'an. The Islamic powers are completely unable either to grasp or accept such a state and, whatever some of their representatives may now be saying, they are ultimately committed to the total destruction of Israel.

Whenever Israel has emerged victorious from war, it has been said that her success was due to American support and financial aid. But this kind of reasoning is in fact illogical because, between them, the Arab nations are among the richest in the world. They influence world events through their hold on the price of oil. The argument then goes on that Israel's strength depends on American weaponry. There will certainly come a time when even this will be withdrawn, and Israel will stand alone. It will be then that the hostile powers will attack.

The threat to Israel stems not so much from the Islamic revival as from the Islamic revolution. The revolution is the violent, dark side of the Islamic revival.

––––––––––

The Ayatollah Khomeini was a brilliant spiritual leader in the Muslim world. He spearheaded the Islamic revolution and he led it for over four decades. His ultimate goal was to bring every nation in the world into submission to Islam. His short-term goal was to bring the Islamic states back to a pure form of fundamentalist religion, led by theocratic government.

In between these two goals, his unshakable aim was to

"liberate" Jerusalem and destroy the Jewish state. He repeatedly stated this objective.

Khomeini first preached his revolutionary program over 40 years ago. It had five stages:

1. Iran must become a theocratic, fundamentalist, and puritan Islamic state. (When the revolution in Iran was successful, and the Israeli embassy in Teheran was transferred to the PLO, Khomeini said, ". . . this is the first stage in the liberation of Jerusalem.")

2. Iraq: from the outbreak of the Iran-Iraq War, Khomeini was repeatedly saying, ". . . This is the next stage in the liberation of Jerusalem."

3. Saudi Arabia, Jordan, Syria, and Egypt are to become theocratic, fundamentalist, puritan Islamic states.

4. The liberation of Jerusalem and the annihilation of the Jewish nation.

5. The conquest of the nations of the world for Islam.

The most remarkable element in Khomeini's preaching was that there were times when he actually mentioned Israel by name. Other Islamic leaders and theologians *try* to ignore Israel. To them she has no right to exist. They ask themselves, "How can Allah be behind the creation of a Jewish state?" When the Israeli delegate to the United Nations gets up to speak, the Arab leaders leave. They do not do so out of pique or bad manners but because of their whole reasoning about Israel. They argue something like this: "The Israeli delegate is a nobody, representing nothing, so why listen to a nobody saying something about nothing?" This attitude also explains the Muslim insistence on any negotiation with Israel being conducted through a third party. Anwar Sadat of Egypt was murdered because he made a direct agreement with Israel.

The Islamic revolution tolerates no opposition. Muslims

accept the teaching of the Qur'an which states that Jews and Christians can be tolerated only as long as they submit themselves to Islam and do not challenge the Qur'an as Allah's final word, or Muhammad as his last and greatest prophet.[31]

The revolution which began in Iran will not end, even though Khomeini has died, for he was merely one interpreter of the history and destiny of Islam. Others have already taken his place.

What about Syria? Today this country is heavily armed and fully prepared to attack Israel. But the land of Syria, as we understand it, is not mentioned in Ezekiel 38. This may be because Syria was part of a much larger territory when Ezekiel made his prophecy. If Syria should attack Israel, it is possible that this could happen before the events described in Ezekiel 38 and 39.

Syria has territorial ambitions, and she dreams of a "Greater Syria" matching in size the earlier provinces of the Roman and Ottoman empires (Luke 2:2). Its boundaries would include Syria, Jordan, Lebanon, and Israel. The peoples of these countries would be allowed some autonomy but would no longer be citizens of independent states. But the promise of God to Abraham, Isaac, and Jacob remains:

> *On the same day the LORD made a covenant with Abram, saying: "To your descendants I have given this land, from the river of Egypt to the great river, the River Euphrates..."* (Genesis 15:18).

> *He is the LORD our God; His judgments are in all the earth. He has remembered His covenant forever, the word which He commanded, for a thousand generations, the covenant which He made with Abraham, and His oath to Isaac, and confirmed it to Jacob for a statute, to Israel for an everlasting covenant, saying, "To you I will give*

> *the land of Canaan as the allotment of your inheritance," when they were but few in number, indeed very few, and strangers in it* (Psalm 105:7-12).

Because of this, confrontation is inevitable. God, in vindication of His holy name, will reveal Himself to Israel in the sight of the nations of the world. When He has given victory to Israel, the very legitimacy of Islam will be at stake. As Islam realizes this, a vacuum will be created in the Muslim world. Those who have been trusting in Allah will deeply ponder the question of whether Islam is truly a revelation of the God of Abraham. The true believers will then see their prayers for Muslims answered. God's "blessing out of Zion," from Israel, will reach the Muslim world. Although the Scriptures clearly show that God's *covenant* promises are for Israel, God has also made promises to the descendants of Ishmael (Genesis 17:20; Isaiah 19:16-25).

All these events happening within and around Israel will be a visible, overwhelming lesson from God for an Islamic world which has been so hard to reach with the gospel. The combination of the founding of a Jewish state, the safekeeping of Israel through five major wars, and the victory in the Gog-Magog war will be powerful lessons indeed. This war, the last attack of Islam against Israel, which will end in such a destructive defeat for the enemies of the Jewish nation, will spell the end of the armies of Communism and Islam (Ezekiel 38:18-23; 39:1-22).

Throughout the Islamic world, hundreds of thousands of men and women will be seeking for an answer. They will turn to the Word of God and come to understand the prophetic Scriptures—and they will discover who God really is.

8

Who Is God?

When God reveals Himself in all His majesty, and delivers Israel, it will at last be seen that the events in the Middle East concern not only the people and the land of Israel, as well as the city of Jerusalem and the Temple Mount; the heart of the matter is *the honor and glory of God*, revealed in His Son, in His Name, and in His Word.

We have already seen how God revealed Himself in His Son, and how Muhammad denies this revelation absolutely. According to Scripture, whoever knows the Son knows the Father (John 14:6-9), and whoever does not know the Son of God cannot know the Father, for God is ONE.

In the Qur'an, Muhammad's God is neither father nor son. Because Muhammad so fiercely resisted the God of the Bible, who reveals Himself as Father and as Son, and presented himself, Muhammad, as the paraclete, he could never have known God. Neither could God have made Himself known through Muhammad as His "last prophet." Because of this, Islam cannot be God's highest final revelation, for that revelation is in His Son.

It is also written in the Scriptures that the *paracletos*, God's Spirit, both glorifies and proclaims Jesus (John 16:12-15). That Muhammad never did this is further evidence that he cannot have known the God of the Bible.

It is in the Son that mankind received the Word of God:

In the beginning was the Word, and the Word was with God, and the Word was God (John 1:1).

It is through this Word that God has made known His name.

The Name

When Shakespeare's Juliet asks, "What's in a name?" she is voicing a certain wisdom, which the Bible calls "the wisdom of men." In the Bible, a person's name not only indicates the essence of his character, but it also gives him his identity. A person might be described by his origin, his outward appearance, his individual characteristics, and his activities, but more than one individual might answer to the same description.

In past centuries, when people spoke about "God" in Western Christendom, it was understood that they meant the God of the Bible. In these days, when we are being confronted by a multitude of "strange gods" (who are as active now as they have always been), it is essential that we express ourselves accurately when we talk about the God of the Holy Scriptures. If we want to know who a person is, we must know his name. If people want to know who God is, they must also know His name.

It was God who took the initiative and revealed Himself. In the distant past of eternity, at a specific moment in time, He spoke. We would never have known about Him had He not chosen to speak from the very beginning of time. By His speaking, He created. God spoke, and it came into being (Genesis 1:1-3; John 1:1-3).

For since the creation of the world His invisible attributes are clearly seen, being understood by the things that are made, even His eternal power and Godhead . . . (Romans 1:20).

We could not have come to know God's name had He not, as it were, introduced Himself to us personally, and made Himself known to mankind by speaking through the mouth of His prophets. As in human society, an introduction can lead on to a much deeper relationship. God revealed more of Himself in the relationships He had with men such as Enoch, Noah, Abraham, Isaac, and Jacob. He came closer and closer to us. In His friendship with Abraham, God committed Himself to a covenant which He confirmed with a solemn oath. God swore this oath on Himself, as there was none higher than He (Genesis 22:16,17; Hebrews 6:13,14). In His covenant with Abraham, God promised that He would give him both descendants and land. He also promised that He would reveal Himself completely through the descendants of Abraham, Isaac, and Jacob (see Genesis 12:1-3).

> *. . . for in Isaac your seed shall be called* (Genesis 21:12b).

In the Old Testament, the story of how God went on making Himself known reached its climax on Mount Sinai, when Moses was given the law; but God actually revealed Himself to Moses much earlier, when He appeared to him in the burning bush. It is sad that the early chapters of Exodus receive relatively little attention, because in them is described one of the greatest of God's acts. This was His calling of Moses, when God entrusted him with the task of leading the children of Israel out of their slavery in Egypt.

When Moses asks God how he can tell the people who was sending him to them, he asks:

> *. . . When I come to the children of Israel and say to them, "The God of your fathers has sent me to you," and they say to me, "What is His name?" what shall I say to them?*

And God answers:

> *I AM WHO I AM. . . . And He said, "Thus you shall say to the children of Israel, 'I AM has sent me to you' "* (Exodus 3:13,14).

In the next verse God speaks His name:

> *Thus you shall say to the children of Israel: "The LORD God of your fathers, the God of Abraham, the God of Isaac, and the God of Jacob, has sent me to you. This is My name forever, and this is My memorial to all generations"* (Exodus 3:15).

In this last passage God reveals His own name. He confirms it later in these words:

> *. . . I am the LORD. I appeared to Abraham, to Isaac, and to Jacob as God Almighty, but by My name JaHWeH I was not known to them* (Exodus 6:2,3).

Until this point God had only been known as "God." In Genesis 17:1 He speaks to Abraham: *"I am Almighty God."* In Genesis 28:3 Isaac speaks to his son Jacob: *"May God Almighty bless you. . . ."* In Genesis 35:11 God speaks to Jacob: *". . . I am God Almighty. . . ."* And in Genesis 43:14 Jacob speaks to his sons: *". . . may God Almighty give you mercy. . . ."* (The word LORD [JaHWeH] is found before the Exodus account—for example, in Genesis 13:4—but there is no discrepancy here, since Moses wrote the book of Genesis.)

"God" is not the name of the God of the Bible. The word "god" indicates "a god," as opposed to an angel, man, animal, plant, or thing. The word is also used in Scripture to refer to idols. There are countless such "gods" in the Bible, referred to as "false gods," "strange gods," or "idols." The word "god" tells us very little unless it is qualified in some way. As it stands, it is simply a common noun and should not be confused with a proper, personal name.

The God of the Bible is often addressed as "Lord"—in Hebrew, *Adonai*. This means "Lord" or "Sir," and it is used much as a title might be used. It indicates that the person being addressed is entitled to some considerable respect.

The God of the Bible, the Creator of heaven and earth, is a living Being. He has made man in His own image and likeness. He has a proper name, which He made known to Israel through Moses.* This name of God is I AM WHO I AM, or in Hebrew, JaHWeH.

The Bible uses three main words for God, and it is the importance of this proper name, JaHWeH, which we now need to consider:

Language	Common Name	Title	Proper Name
English	god	lord	I AM WHO I AM
Hebrew	elohim	adonai	JaHWeH

In biblical times the name JaHWeH was spoken, but later its use in speech became less common. As time went by, when the name written as JaHWeH was spoken it was pronounced as Adonai. In other words, God's proper name, JaHWeH, was replaced by "Adonai," which is merely a title.

---

* If the name JaHWeH was not known to Abraham, Isaac, and Jacob, then it cannot have been known to Ishmael, nor to his sons Nebajoth, Kedar, Abdeel, and their brothers (see Genesis 25:12ff.). Ishmael's sons went to live between Havila and Sur, east of Egypt, the region which is now Saudi Arabia. This is also the region where Muhammad's predecessors, the Quraish tribe, originated.

The Torah (the Law) does not forbid the speaking of God's proper name. The commandment is that it should not be "taken in vain" or used idly. But the term Adonai came to be used by custom, and those who translated the Hebrew Scriptures into English followed the Jewish example and substituted the capitalized form LORD where JaHWeH was written.* (There are, in fact, no capital letters in Hebrew, nor are there any vowels. The *a* and *e* inserted into JaHWeH in the Roman script are there to guide us as to pronunciation.)

These same translators followed Jewish tradition as closely as possible and replaced the four consonants J H W H by the four letters L O R D. This actually detracts from the true meaning of God's name. The French translation, L'Eternel, the Eternal One, is perhaps closer to the meaning of the original Hebrew.

This substitution of LORD for the proper, given name of God, JaHWeH, has not been without consequence, for both Judaism and Christianity have been deprived of precious truth. I am not necessarily pleading here for a change in practice, but rather for an understanding of the seriousness of this loss.

A good example of the confusion which results from a wrong rendering of the name of God is to be found in the expression "The name of the Lord." Let us look at the following verses from the Bible:

> *O LORD, our Lord, how excellent is Your name in all the earth!* (Psalm 8:1).

> *... that men may know that You, whose name alone is the LORD, are the Most High over all the earth* (Psalm 83:18).

---

* In most English Bibles if the Name JaHWeH follows the title Lord, it is written "Lord GOD"—as in Amos 3:7 and Ezekiel 37:21.

O LORD God of hosts, who is mighty like You, O LORD? . . . For who in the heavens can be compared to the LORD? (Psalm 89:8,6a).

I am the LORD, that is My name . . . (Isaiah 42:8).

Our Redeemer, the LORD of hosts is His name (Isaiah 47:4).

The name of the LORD is a strong tower . . . (Proverbs 18:10).

When we come to read verses like these, we cannot help but ask ourselves, "Who is God?" We then have to ask, "What is His name?" These are crucial questions. In order to answer them properly, we must look at some of the problems concerned with the translation of the Bible from the original Hebrew.

There are two main points which confuse the issue. First, where the phrase *". . . of the LORD"* occurs in the above verses, the genitive form ("of the . . .") merely has an explanatory function. The words "of the . . ." in front of LORD are not only superfluous but they are an incorrect translation of the Hebrew. The strictly correct rendering should be "The name LORD."

Second, it still remains unclear who the "LORD" is, until the phrase normally rendered as "the name of the LORD" is correctly translated as "the name JaHWeH." To give an example from the above verses, a better rendering of Proverbs 18:10 would be *"The name JaHWeH* [LORD] *is a strong tower. . . ."*

This careless handling of the original Hebrew has led to some peculiar developments. There is much preaching and teaching based on the following words: Elohim, Adonai, El Elion, JaHWeH Jireh, Rophecha, Nissi, Kaddish, Shalom, Roi, Sabaoth, and Shamma. These mean, respectively, "god," "lord," "god of the ages," "JaHWeH provides,"

"your healer," "my banner," "holy," "peace," "my shepherd," ["LORD of . . ."] "hosts" and ["the LORD is . . ."]
"there." These words are used as if they were each different
names for God. While teaching along this line is sincerely
meant, it is in fact erroneous and confusing. It has even been
said that JaHWeH Shamma—"The LORD is there"—is a
name for God. In fact, it is the name of the city of Jerusalem
(see Ezekiel 48:35). And the word "Rophecha" means
"your physician" or "healer." But "healer" refers to the
function of healing which He, God, fulfills; it is not His
name. Similarly, Jireh means "he will provide." But God's
provision for our needs refers to His activity on our behalf.
Again, it is not His proper name.

The all-embracing name of God, His proper name, is
JaHWeH.[32] The descriptions which God gives of Himself,
such as "I am the First and the Last, Creator, Maker, Savior,
Shepherd, Rock, and Physician," should be considered as
facets or partial revelations of who He is. While God's
revelation of Himself as Father, Son and Holy Spirit is the
most important of all, even these are not His names. They
are expressions which convey His character and His functions and actions in relation to mankind and to His whole
creation.

Just as some people ascribe to God functions and activities which are not names, so Islam does with Allah.
Muhammad assigned 99 "names" to Allah, but there is no
proper name among them; they are only attributes. For
example, Allah is known as "the merciful, the king, the
provider, the distributor, the clever One, the counter, the
first One, the last One, the independent, the usurer, the
inheritor," and so on.

When a Muslim is asked, "Who is your God?" he will
answer, "Allah." When asked, "What is his name?" his
answer is also "Allah."

The word "Allah" is made up of the article "al" (the) and the common noun "ilah" (God). Thus the word "allah" means "the God." It is the Arabic equivalent of the Hebrew word *ha-elohim*. Just as the Muslim uses the word "Allah" for his God, so Christian Arabs use "Allah" when they are talking about the God of the Bible. When the Islamic creed states that "Allah is God," this is the same as saying, "The god is god" or "god is the god."

Language	Common Name	Title	Proper Name
English	god	lord	I AM WHO I AM
Hebrew	elohim	adonai	JaHWeH
Arabic	allah (ilah)	————	————

The above table shows that "Allah" is not technically a proper name.

There has long been discussion in Islam over the "hundredth name of Allah," which some say is "the Exalted Name" which no one knows. But the God of Israel did reveal His name: *"The LORD [JaHWeH] . . . this is My name forever. . . ."* (Exodus 3:15). And Jesus prayed:

> *I have manifested thy name to the men whom thou gavest me out of the world. . . .*
>
> *. . . .keep them in thy name, which thou hast given me. . . .*
>
> *I have made known to them thy name . . .* (John 17:6,11,26 RSVB).

God's own name is JaHWeH. It is the name He gave to Israel when He delivered them out of Egypt and made His covenant with them on Mount Sinai. It is the name He gave them when He chose them as a people for His own possession and entered into a marriage relationship with them. This is why He said to them:

> *I am the* LORD *your God, who brought you out. . . .*
>
> *You shall have no other gods before Me. . . .*
>
> *For I, the* LORD *your God, am a jealous God* (Exodus 20:2,3,5).

The greatness of the God of that name had to be made known again and again to the people of Israel, and through them to the peoples of the surrounding nations.

When Moses told Jethro, his father-in-law, all that JaH-weH had done, Jethro replied, *"Now I know that the* LORD *is greater than all the gods . . ."* (Exodus 18:11).

The same name was "in the Angel" who led the people out of Egypt:

> *Behold, I send an Angel before you, to keep you in the way and to bring you into the place which I have prepared. Beware of Him and obey His voice . . . for My name is in Him* (Exodus 23:20, 21).

In Jericho, Rahab the harlot said to the spies:

> *For we have heard how the* LORD *[JaHWeH] dried up the water of the Red Sea for you. . . . And as soon as we heard these things, our hearts melted; neither did there remain any more courage in anyone because of you, for JaHWeH your God, He is God in heaven above and on earth beneath. Now therefore, I beg you, swear to me by JaHWeH, since I have shown you kindness . . . and deliver our lives from death* (Joshua 2:10-13).

Ruth, the Moabite girl, promised to be faithful to her mother-in-law Naomi, and she even invoked a judgment from JaHWeH on herself in the event of her unfaithfulness. It was of this God that she said:

. . . and your God, my God (Ruth 1:16).

Naaman, the Syrian general, acknowledged that his healing came from the God of Israel:

Indeed, now I know that there is no God in all the earth, except in Israel (2 Kings 5:15).

Naaman went on to say that he would no longer offer burnt sacrifices or meat-offerings to any god other than JaHWeH. He went on to express further the hope that Elisha's God would grant him mercy when he had to accompany his master into the temple of the false god Rimmon. While supporting his master as he bowed down to his god, Naaman too would have to bow down to this idol (2 Kings 5:15-19).

———————

Not only the Gentile nations but Israel too had to be reminded time and again that JaHWeH, and none other, was the God of Israel. Who will set fire to the altar built by Elijah, the baals or JaHWeH? God's response to Elijah is powerfully shown on Mount Carmel, where Elijah prayed:

JaHWeH God of Abraham, Isaac, and Israel, let it be known this day that You are God in Israel. . . . Hear me, JaHWeH, hear me, that this people may know that You, JaHWeH, are God . . . (1 Kings 18:36,37).

The fire from JaHWeH fell down and consumed the burnt offering and licked up the water in the trench. And when the people saw this they fell on their faces and said:

JaHWeH, Hu ha elohim! JaHWeH, Hu ha elohim! (JaHWeH, He is God! JaHWeH, He is God!)

For centuries we have clung to the impersonal words "God" and "LORD" instead of using God's proper name. Because of this we have deprived ourselves of much precious teaching from the Bible.

> *You shall fear JaHWeH your God and serve Him, and shall take oaths in His name. You shall not go after other gods, the gods of the peoples who are all around you* (Deuteronomy 6:13,14).

Words spoken in the name of God should be regarded as the greatest and most authoritative way of speaking that can ever be. This was the way the prophets of Israel spoke.

The time will come when the nations of the world will learn to speak in a different way. They too will learn to "swear by the name of the LORD." The time will come when there will no longer be a choice between making an oath or an affirmation, as in a law court, for people will swear by the God of truth. The ineffectual phrases "I promise . . ." and ". . . so help me God" will become obsolete.

Through the mouth of Jeremiah, God tells us how this transformation will take place. As always, God teaches us through His own people:

> *Thus says JaHWeH: Against all My evil neighbors who touch the inheritance which I have caused My people Israel to inherit—behold, I will pluck them out of their land and pluck out the house of Judah from among them. Then it shall be, after I have plucked them out, that I will return and have compassion on them and bring them back, every-one to his heritage and everyone to his land. And it shall be, if they will diligently learn the ways of My people, to swear by My name, "As JaHWeH lives," as they taught My people to swear by Baal, then they shall be established in the midst of My people* (Jeremiah 12:14-16).

For the past 40 years it has been evident that God is again having compassion on His people Israel and bringing them back to His land.

In Israel, too, something new will take place. We have already seen how God made His own name, ЈаНWеН, known, and how He put it upon Israel and joined Himself to His people through the miraculous exodus from Egypt. ЈаНWеН was the God of that event, and He foretells through Jeremiah how He will link His name once more with them by bringing about a similar event, a second exodus:

> *Therefore, behold, the days are coming, says the LORD, that they shall no longer say, "As the LORD lives who brought up the children of Israel from the land of Egypt," but "As the LORD lives who brought up and led the descendants of the house of Israel from the north country and from all the countries where I had driven them." And they shall dwell in their own land* (Jeremiah 23:7,8).

The exodus of the descendants of the Jewish people from the north country (from the Soviet Union and from the whole dispersion) remains one of the prophetic promises which until now has been only partially fulfilled. ЈаНWеН, who delivered His people from Egypt, will be seen to be the very same God who will set His people free from the Soviet Union.

Israel traces her existence as a nation back to three events in her history: God's deliverance of the children of Israel from Egypt, God's giving to them of His name, and God's betrothal to His people by the covenant made at Mount Sinai. The promised exodus from the north will be just such an event, to which God will once again link His name.

It was the prophet Jeremiah who was called to foretell this great exodus from the north. While he considered himself to be too young to be God's messenger, ЈаНWеН confirmed to him that he would truly be speaking in the name of the God of Israel. God showed him the branch of an almond tree, and He asked Jeremiah:

> *"Jeremiah, what do you see?" And I said, "I see a rod of almond." Then the LORD said to me, "You have seen well, for I am watching over my word to perform it"* (Jeremiah 1:11,12 RSVB).

There is a play on the Hebrew words for "almond" and "watching" in these two verses which is missed in translation. The almond tree is *sha-ked* in the Hebrew, and the word for "watching" (which also has the meaning of "being ready") is *sho-ked*. The root letters of "almond" in Hebrew are *s*, *k*, and *d*, and these same letters are the root letters of the expression which means "diligently watching until the completion of a task." They also convey the ideas of speed and alertness.

In Israel, the almond tree is the first of the trees to blossom in the spring. It is always "ready and waiting." It is a harbinger of spring and it announces the coming summer. In the same way, God Himself will diligently and speedily see that His Word will be completely fulfilled. Jeremiah 23:7,8, which we have just read, is one of the most powerful Scriptures containing two of the three elements through which God expresses His commitment to His people. These are His name and His Word.

The Word

> *For as the rain comes down and the snow from heaven, and do not return there but water the earth, and make it bring forth and bud, that it may give seed to the sower and bread to the eater, so shall My word be that goes forth from My mouth; it shall not return to Me void, but it shall*

*accomplish what I please, and it shall prosper in
the thing for which I sent it* (Isaiah 55:10,11).

In these verses from Isaiah, God explains how His Word,
once spoken by Him, completes a circular journey of whatever distance and then returns to Him completely fulfilled.
God Himself guarantees His Word and its fulfillment, for
He and His Word are one and the same (John 1:1). Isaiah
says that "*. . . the word of our God stands forever*" (Isaiah
40:8). This means that once God has spoken His Word, the
fulfillment is certain.

The uniqueness of the Bible lies in its prophetic element,
which distinguishes it from all other religious books. Allah
does not speak in this way. The prophetic voice is absent
from the Qur'an.

While for mankind time may seem to pass very slowly,
the psalmist assures us that God's Word "runs very swiftly"
(Psalm 147:15). His Word, spoken in the distant past, soon
becomes reality. Sometimes its fulfillment goes unnoticed,
and sometimes it is hidden, but at other times it bursts out
like a sudden explosion. Peter writes:

*We also have the prophetic word made more sure,
which you do well to heed as a light that shines in a
dark place . . .* (2 Peter 1:19).

In these days, when even the world sees something of the
fulfillment of the prophetic Word of God, many churches
keep these parts of Scripture hidden. Many of today's theologians and preachers feel that great care needs to be exer-
cised when it comes to explaining prophecy. And in one
sense they are right: Playing with dates and presumptuous
handling of the prophetic Scriptures are confusing and
unscriptural.

Nearly 2000 years ago, Jesus' interpretation of the Scriptures did not readily fit into the theology of His day, and dogma blocked the way to the living Lord. Because of this, the spiritual leaders did not recognize Jesus at His first coming. In the same way, in our own day people have shackled the Word of God and tried to render it powerless.

In the traditional teaching of Christianity, the church has taken the place of Israel. So how does "the church" explain what is written in the Scriptures about the return of the Jews to the land of Israel, in the light of the events of world history, both past and present? There are three main views on this whole subject:

1. The return of the Jews to "the Land" was fulfilled during their return from the Babylonian captivity.[33]

2. The present state of Israel and the continuing return of Jews to "the Land" is merely a "Zionist-inspired accident of history."

3. The humanist viewpoint: that the Jews, in order to have some security in the world, and bearing in mind such events as the Holocaust, are at least entitled to a "safe refuge."

Because "the church" has applied the biblical prophecies to herself, they have obviously had to be spiritualized. But the first essential of true biblical exegesis is a literal application of the text. Such literal interpretation, when related to the Jewish people and the land of Israel, does not accord with the established theology of Roman Catholicism or, indeed, of much Protestant theology.

The "spiritualization" (nonliteralization) of the prophetic Scriptures has created a stumbling block in the way of a simple understanding of the Bible. Yet such a wrong use of the prophetic Scriptures by some people, and the ensuing results, cannot justify our neglect or ignorance of the prophetic Word of God. Whatever one may make of these Scriptures, they remain as written for those for whom God intended them. In fulfillment of Amos 9:11, it is clear that, in our own day, God has begun to restore the fallen tent of David, and to repair its broken places and ruins. (See also Acts 15:16,17.)

Preaching which does not see the restoration of the Jewish people to the land of Israel as a prophetic event damages not only Israel but also the church. Just as traditional Jewish theology prevented Israel from recognizing their Messiah nearly 2000 years ago, so much Christian doctrine today prevents people from recognizing the signs of the times and the events which indicate the second coming of Jesus:

> *Then He also said to the multitudes, "When you see a cloud rising out of the west, immediately you say, 'A shower is coming'; and so it is. And when you see the south wind blow, you say, 'There will be hot weather'; and there is.... You can discern the face of the sky and of the earth, but how is it you do not discern this time?"* (Luke 12:54-56).

In environmental pollution and other catastrophes and disasters, man is prepared to see symptoms of a possible approaching end, but all too many people refuse to accept the biblical signs as signals of the end times. They reject the link between the things the Scriptures say and their actual fulfillment.

> *... If you had known ... the things that make for your peace! But now they are hidden from your eyes ... because you did not know the time of your visitation* (Luke 19:42,44).

It is not the detailed explanation and application of each prophetic passage of Scripture which is important. What is vital to understand is that the whole prophetic biblical word is a blueprint for the future of Israel, the nations, and the world. Allowing the Bible to speak for itself is more persuasive than any preaching. God's Word announces the very things we now see being fulfilled before our very eyes.

God, revealing Himself as LORD, JaHWeH, the King of Jacob, says:

> *"Present your case," says the LORD. "Bring forth your strong reasons," says the King of Jacob. "Let them bring forth and show us what will happen; let them show the former things, what they were, that we may consider them, and know the latter end of them; or declare to us things to come. Show the things that are to come hereafter, that we may know that you are gods; yes, do good or do evil, that we may be dismayed and see it together. Indeed you are nothing, and your work is nothing . . ."* (Isaiah 41:21-24a).

In this challenge, God sets His seal, as it were, on His own authenticity. He is the God who tells us ahead of time what He proposes to do, and He then does what He has said. In Isaiah 47:12,13 He issues a further challenge to man, this time regarding man's expectations from "other gods":

> *Stand now with your enchantments and the multitude of your sorceries . . . . You are wearied in the multitude of your counsels; let now the astrologers, the stargazers, and the monthly prognosticators stand up and save you from these things that shall come upon you.*

Who then has the last word? It is the One who says:

I am JaHWeH, that is My name; and My glory I will not give to another, nor My praise to graven images (Isaiah 42:8).

He, JaHWeH, is the first and the last, the God who is beyond both time and space. He surveys the past, the present, and the future. In His hand He has the beginning and the end. He sets up the measure by which the true God may be known. His challenge to false gods comes yet again: *"Show the things that are to come hereafter, that we may know that you are gods."* He alone knows what is to come. Who is He who can do such a thing?

Who declared it from the beginning, that we might know, and before time, that we might say, "He is right"? There was none who declared it, none who proclaimed, none who heard your words. I first have declared it to Zion (Isaiah 41:26,27a RSVB).

God is saying, "I am the first One to have done this, and I told . . . Zion." Once again He introduces Himself by saying, "I am JaHWeH, the God of Zion, the God of Israel."

Remember the former things of old; for I am God, and there is no other; I am God, and there is none like me, declaring the end from the beginning and from ancient times things not yet done, saying, "My counsel shall stand, and I will accomplish all my purpose" . . . I have spoken, and I will bring it to pass; I have purposed, and I will do it (Isaiah 46:9-11 RSVB).

Who is the only true God? Who is God?

> *Thus says the LORD, the King of Israel and his Redeemer, the LORD of hosts: "I am the first and I am the last; besides me there is no god. Who is like me?"* (Isaiah 44:6,7a RSVB).

The answer comes from David:

> *O LORD, there is none like You, nor is there any God besides You, according to all that we have heard with our ears. And who is like Your people Israel, the one nation on the earth whom God went to redeem for Himself as a people—to make for Yourself a name?* (1 Chronicles 17:20,21).

Epilogue

*E*urope has only the gracious protection of God to thank for the fact that, on two occasions in the past, she has been saved from Islamic domination. It is therefore utterly incomprehensible that for the past 30 years or so her gates have been opened wide to Islam.

This is not simply the result of economic factors. There are many spiritual leaders in Europe who are quite deliberately doing all they can to unite Judaism, Christianity, and Islam, with the intention of bringing all three under one roof.

The Swiss Roman Catholic theologian Hans Küng believes that Muhammad should no longer be considered a false prophet. According to Küng, Muhammad's zeal in bringing hundreds of millions of people to faith in one God should now be taken seriously.[34]

History teaches us that any ruler seeking to centralize his authority over a wide area can only do so by introducing uniformity at every level of society.

The Bible tells us, particularly in the books of Daniel and Revelation, that a world ruler will reign shortly before the return of Jesus Christ to the earth. This ruler will only be able to bring unity to his government when all the world's religions are joined together in one. It would seem that the Roman Catholic Church will form an important pillar in this new structure. It is no coincidence that for centuries she has called herself "Civitas Dei," God's state on earth, or *oeucumene*. This Greek word implies "the whole inhabited world" or the "world church." It is also no coincidence that for several decades now the Roman Catholic Church has led the way in promoting dialogue with Islam and other religions.

In the light of biblical prophecy, it is clear that Canterbury, Geneva, and Wittenburg will find their way back to Rome. Together they will strive to achieve a single goal: the future amalgamation of all religions to form one world faith.

There is even now a network uniting all streams of religious thought throughout the world. It is known as the New Age movement. It teaches that man already has the divine within him. God is not transcendent, "something or someone" beyond and outside man. Rather, "god has always lived in man." This mode of thinking lies at the heart of many pagan religions. The Bible tells us that from the very beginning man had a desire to be equal with God. The attempt of man to attain equality with God resulted in his fall and alienation from God.

Within the pantheistic framework of the teaching that "God is in all things," a god without a name fits very well. Islam has a god without a name. If the attempts to bring together Judaism, Christianity and Islam are successful, then Islam, in its West-European guise, could provide the bridge leading all three of these faiths into the spirituality of the New Age.

According to New Age teaching and spirituality, "God" is considered to be a universal power or "force," and it is held that everyone possesses the divine "spark" within him. Man is on the way to becoming his own god.

It cannot be disputed, as Hans Küng has said, that Muhammad has been extremely successful in the promotion of faith in one "God." But, as we have seen, he has brought people to a faith in a "God" who is not the Judeo-Christian God, the God of the Bible. Now well-entrenched in Europe,

Islam has made more inroads into people's consciousness than ever before. It could be an important part of the growing belief in the world ruler, or Antichrist, a title which actually means "instead of Christ," or the counterfeit Christ.

Now that it has been clearly shown that Allah is not the God of the Bible, we must realize how seriously theologians like Küng and others are leading people astray. Verkuyl voices his deep concern when he writes:

> There is more and more speculative thought in certain forms of "theology of religions" about the "place of Islam in God's plan of salvation." I want to illustrate this point. Since the publication of the decree "Nostra Aetate," formulated by the Second Vatican Council, there are many Roman Catholic theologians who, under the influence both of this decree and the theological arguments of Karl Rahner, Raymond Panikkar, H.R. Schlette and others, now believe that Islam is one of the "incomplete ways of salvation and as such it has a place in God's plan of salvation for mankind." Karl Rahner argues:

> > If God wants to show his grace to all, then that grace must take on a socio-historical form if it is to become truly available to every man. The most acceptable mediating channels for this mercy are the religions. The religions are the depositories of grace, each offering ways of salvation and so in a positive sense they should be included in God's plan of salvation.[35]

Using these ideas, certain Christian theologians assert that there are many different ways to salvation, all of them different from the way which leads to Golgotha. These ways vary from people to people and from culture to culture, and they are historically determined. Each and every religion is supposed to be a mediating channel for grace and salvation. We must assume that Rahner and Panikkar and the others mean by "salvation" that which is promised in Scripture rather than the panoramic view offered by other religions. If this were not so, they would not be pleading in favor of "many routes" to the one ultimate goal.

———

What is grace? What is salvation? Salvation is the gift of God. Grace points to the "form" of His gift, while salvation is its content. Grace is a word which shows us how God behaves toward us. Salvation is not simply everlasting life, for this is also preached in other religions. The Bible tells of immortality for all, the just and the unjust, but the salvation offered by the God of Israel is everlasting life *in His presence*. The alternative is to be separated from Him forever and to remain living outside of Him, in nothing.

Separation between God and man came about through man's fall in the Garden of Eden. But it was on the cross that God allowed His Son to experience that separation and awful abandonment:

> . . . *My God, My God, why have You forsaken Me?*
> (Matthew 27:46).

By giving Himself as a sacrifice, Jesus brought about the reconciliation of man to God, and the separation between them was broken down. All those who accept Jesus' sacrifice and allow Him to do His atoning work within them, by asking Him into their hearts, are reconciled to God. The heart of biblical salvation is forgiveness of sin and everlasting life with God, with all the blessings for man, society, and creation which follow.

This is only a bare outline of God's full salvation. There is still much which has not yet been revealed to us (1 Corinthians 2:9).

At this point we must state clearly that truly biblical salvation is available only through Jesus and His sacrifice for us on the cross. Salvation is nothing less than the reconciliation He effected for us. It makes nonsense of Scripture for anyone to claim that salvation is available apart from the atoning death of Jesus. Grace means that God is offering to us, freely, the salvation wrought by His Son, Jesus Christ. It is free! It is for all those who seek it, and who reach out and ask for it.

To return to Karl Rahner and the other theologians. It seems that they are attempting to equate two biblical texts. These are "For the grace of God has appeared for the salvation of all men . . ." and "For he makes his sun rise on the evil and on the good, and he sends rain on the just and on the unjust." But there is a false analogy here. God's salvation cannot be compared with the relationship of man to natural phenomena such as the sun and the rain.

These theologians have launched a method of reasoning which contains a number of inconsistent and contradictory elements.

What some theologians are saying today is that the revelation of God in the Scriptures may be compared and even equated with religions such as Buddhism, Hinduism, Islam, and others. Rahner pleads that Islam offers an "almost equal way of salvation." He argues that these various other ways should be accepted within the context, framework, and character of the history and culture of their adherents. But in relation to Islam (to take the example with which we are particularly concerned) this line of reasoning is both inconsistent and ambiguous.

In the Bible there are numerous references to the God of Israel in contrast to all other gods:

> *I am the LORD your God, who brought you out of the land of Egypt, out of the house of bondage. You shall have no other gods before Me* (Exodus 20:2,3).

> *...for they went and served other gods and worshiped them, gods that they did not know and that He had not given to them. Then the anger of the LORD was aroused against this land...* (Deuteronomy 29:26,27a).

> *...for the LORD your God, He is God in heaven above and on earth beneath* (Joshua 2:11).

> *Thus says the LORD, the God of Israel, "Your fathers lived of old beyond the Euphrates, ... and they served other gods"* (Joshua 24:2 RSVB).

> *...choose for yourselves this day whom you will serve, whether the gods which your fathers served that were on the other side of the River, or the gods of the Amorites, in whose land you dwell. But as for me and my house, we will serve the LORD* (Joshua 24:15).

Anyone who studies the Bible in any depth to see what it says about the God of Israel is soon overwhelmed by His awesome greatness.

He is God. He is the LORD. He is the One who laid the foundations of the earth and determined her boundaries. He has "stretched out a measuring line" over the earth. He has "set her pillars and established her cornerstone." He has determined the times and seasons for every man, whether king or slave, and He has determined the times and seasons of every power and every kingdom. This God, who is above time and space, in the distant past and for the sake of man created both time and space and then entered this creation.

He spoke, and by His Word everything came into being. By His Word He has revealed Himself. The sound of His voice was heard. He made Himself so that man could hear Him, see Him, and experience Him. He limited Himself so that He could be perceived by the eyes, ears, and hearts of men.

This almighty, majestic God has, for the sake of man, "squeezed" Himself into a specific and limited framework so as to be understood by man.

He has revealed Himself. He has made His name known. He has betrothed Himself to a particular nation, the nation of Israel. He has chosen a place to live.

It sounds almost profane, but He so humbled and diminished Himself that He allowed Himself to be laid in an animal's feeding-trough.

He took on human form, and for about 33 years He lived the life of a man. He has made known His plans and expressed His policy in terms that even we can grasp and calculate, like times, centuries, seasons, and days. He, the Most Holy One, seated above the clouds, has revealed more about Himself and His works than any earthly ruler ever did.

He has limited Himself to this dimension of space and time so that He might come close to man. He has done exactly this with the people of Israel (Psalm 147:19,20; 148:14b).

———————

To use Rahner's terminology, God has for the sake of man placed Himself completely within a sociohistorical framework.

Muhammad has completely broken with this framework. He speaks of the people of Israel as if they were a people no different from any other. He takes biblical events out of their historical context. The city of Jerusalem is not mentioned in the Qur'an, nor is the land of Israel. In contrast with the ways of the God of the Bible, there is no beginning and no end to Allah's dealings with man and the world: Somewhere, sometime, there will be a day of judgment. In Scripture this event is clearly indicated, but in the Qur'an it is only alluded to in vague and threatening terms.

In conclusion, Muhammad attempted to distort the greatness of the mighty God of Israel, the greatness of this God in His being and in His works, which are beyond understanding, has nevertheless been revealed to man. This greatness has become accessible to us. Yet Islam completely removes from biblical faith the very sociohistorical setting for which Rahner pleads. As far as Islam is concerned, Rahner and the other theologians like him consider this religion to be "an almost perfect way of salvation." In saying this, these theologians are doing their best to nullify God's greatest manifestation of Himself in the whole history of creation. But the real resistance to the God of the Bible is in the power struggle which is raging in the spiritual realm above, where the princes of darkness still bitterly oppose the Prince of Israel (Daniel 10:13-21; Ephesians 6:12).

As in biblical times, when Elijah, Hezekiah, Isaiah, and other great men of God did not tolerate any mocking of the LORD God of Israel, so in our day it is unthinkable that the false gods of the nations should be considered equal to the God of Jerusalem (2 Chronicles 32:19).

Who is like unto Thee, JaHWeH of Hosts!

Notes

############################

1. In everyday language a "Christian" is someone who calls him-
    self a "Christian" regardless of the content of his faith. Chris-
    tianity becomes the sum of what these "Christians" believe.

    From the first century these "Christians" have based the
    content of their faith either on more than the Bible or on less than
    the Bible.

    More than the Bible would include, for instance, the Creeds,
    Catechisms and dogmas as well as the writings of other "Chris-
    tians."

    Faith based on less than biblical truth leaves out such themes
    as:

    - the still-to-be fulfilled promises for Israel and the
      Jewish people;

    - the New Covenant having been made with the
      people of Israel;

    - the personal, physical, visible return of Messiah
      Jesus, on the Mount of Olives;

    - the earthly kingdom to begin when Jesus returns as
      King of Israel;

    - Jerusalem to be the earthly capital of that kingdom.

    These themes and more, serve as an integral part of biblical
    revelation. As a result of not rightly dividing the Word of truth,
    these doctrines have been and still are being denied, ignored, or
    opposed.

    For this reason I prefer the term "Biblical Faith" rather than
    "Christianity" when I speak about the content of that faith
    which finds its boundaries only from within the Bible.

    Where the reader finds the term "Christianity" used in this
    book, he should discern its meaning on the basis of the above
    information.

2. Lance Lambert, lecture, *Israel and the Nations* (Jerusalem,
    1986).

3. J. Verkuyl, *Speaking to Muslims About the Gospel* (Kampen, 1985), p. 32.
4. A. Wessels, *Understanding the Qur'an* (Kampen), p. 43.
5. Ibid., p. 48.
6. J. Budd, *Studies on Islam* (Rushden, Northants, 1967), p. 13.
7. Ibid., p. 15.
8. H. Kohlbrugge, *Confrontation with Islam* (The Hague, 1980), pp. 20, 21.
9. J. Verkuyl, op. cit., pp. 20, 21.
10. A. Wessels, op. cit., p. 10.
11. Ibid., p. 11.
12. J. Slomp, "The Qur'an for Christians and other Beginners," in *Trouw*, November 18, 1986.
13. W. Cantwell Smith, cited in J. Verkuyl, op. cit., p. 14.
14. J. Verkuyl, op. cit., p. 48.
15. Ibn Abi Zayd Qarawan, quoted in G. Bergmann, *The Challenge of Islam* ('Le Defi de l'Islam') (Centre de Diffusion Evangelique, Paris), p. 25.
16. J. Verkuyl, op. cit., p. 78.
17. J. Budd, op. cit., p. 24.
18. J. Verkuyl, op. cit., pp. 78, 79.
19. Ibid., p. 58.
20. Cited in G. Bergmann, op. cit., p. 28.
21. Cited in J. Verkuyl, op. cit., p. 84.
22. G. Bergmann, op. cit., p. 31.
23. *Al Islam des Musulmans en Allemagne*, No. 3, 1979.
24. Abd-Al-Masih, *Wer Ist Allah im Islam?* (Villach), p. 32.
25. Ibid., p. 30.
26. Implied here is the *ka'aba* in Mecca, which, according to Islamic tradition, was built by both Abraham and Isma'il (Ishmael). About a thousand years before Christ, the God of Israel, for the first time, allowed a house (the Temple) to be built in Jerusalem for Him and for His name (2 Samuel 7:12). Around 30 A.D., Jesus said that the worship of His God and Father was not restricted to any particular location (John 4:23). Paul confirmed this (Acts 17:24). But in 600 A.D. the Qur'an suddenly asserts that Abraham and Ishmael had built God a holy place 2600 years earlier. This sanctuary is the Ka'aba in Mecca and it is still the Muslims' most holy place. God must be very inconsistent in His plans—or are they really two different gods?

27. J. Wessels, op. cit., p. 110.

28. Ibid., p. 111.

29. Ibid., p. 111.

30. After the war of 1967, the Soviet Union was one of the first nations to call for an unconditional return to the "status quo ante." This is in complete contradiction to its own practice in Eastern Europe. Referring to the situation of the Communist bloc at the end of the Second World War, an article in *Pravda*, on September 2, 1964, stated: "The borders of the state have become sanctified in the efforts of the settlers in the border villages and by the streams of blood which they have had to shed in their defense. A people which had been attacked, and which defended itself and emerged victorious, has the sacred right of establishing for itself such a final political settlement as would permit it to liquidate the sources of aggression . . . a people which has acquired its security with such heavy sacrifice will never agree to restore the old borders." See Carta, *Secure and Recognized Boundaries*, Jerusalem, 1971, p. 27.

    This is a truth which should be applied in the case of Israel, too.

31. I am greatly indebted to Lance Lambert for much of the information on pages 93-95.

32. God made known His name on only one other occasion. This was the name of His Son. *"You shall call His name Yeshua* [Jesus], *for He will save His people from their sins."* This is the name of God become man, the "name under heaven given among men" (Acts 4:12). It is a proper name, and it denotes an action. The Latin form is "Jesus," but only the Hebrew "Yeshua" truly conveys the meaning "salvation." Only this name gives us access to God (Acts 4:12 and John 14:6). The Yeshua side of God is His saving arm stretched out toward mankind. By His very being, and by His word and His works, Yeshua has fully revealed the name of God (John 17:6,11).

33. That "the return from Babylon" does not fulfill the biblical promises concerning the final return of both Israel and Judah to "the Land," is clear from Scripture: Jeremiah 23:7,8; 31:3-14; 32:36-41; 33:7,8; Amos 9:14,15; Isaiah 11:11,12; 43:5,7; Ezekiel 37:1-14,21,22.

    That the "return from Babylon" (538 to 446 B.C.) was not final is clear from history, for the Jews were driven from the land after the destruction of the Temple by the Romans in 70 A.D. The biblical references also make it very clear that the final return of the Jews to Israel will be from countries all over the world.

34. H. Küng, *Christianity and the World Religions* (London: Collins, 1987).
35. Cited in J. Verkuyl, op. cit., p. 131.

GLOSSARY

Abu Talib: Mohammad's uncle.

Allah: The God of Islam.

Ayatollah Khomeini: The main personality behind the revival of fundamentalist Islam in the twentieth century.

Caliph Othman: Muhammad's third successor. He put together the collected words and sayings of Muhammad, which became known as the Qur'an.

Dar-al-Harb: "House of War"—a territory or nation not subject to Islamic law.

Dar-al-Salaam: "House of Peace"—a territory or nation subject to Islamic law.

Diaspora: The Jews "in dispersion," i.e. those living anywhere except in the land of Israel.

Eretz Israel: The land of Israel.

Hadith: Muslim tradition.

Haje (or "Hadj")*:* The pilgrimage to Mecca, which every faithful Muslim should make at least once in his lifetime.

Injil (or "Indjil")*:* Islamic word for the New Testament or Gospels.

Islam: World religion whose founder is Muhammad. The word "Islam" means "submission."

Jihad: The Holy War; a Qur'anic injunction to the faithful Muslim.

Ka'aba: The name of Islam's most holy sanctuary in Mecca. The word means literally "a square building."

Kismet: A Turkish word derived from the Arabic "qismah," meaning "a lot" (in the sense to draw a lot or to choose an option).

Kitab (or "Kitav")*:* Arabic: "book."

Mahdi: The Muslim concept of "the forerunner."

Mansukh: Muslim teaching on the "process of obsolescence" in the Bible.

Masih: An anointed one who travels about—a title linked to Jesus in the Qur'an.

Mecca: A city in Saudi Arabia; the birthplace of Muhammad and the most holy city of Islam.

Messiah: The "Anointed One." The anointing normally preceded the assumption of kingship.

Muhammad (also Mohammed or Mahomet)*:* The founder of the Islamic religion. Born in Mecca, 570 A.D.

Muharraf: An Arabic term for the corruption of a biblical text.

Muslim: A follower of Islam; a worshiper of Allah.

Nabi: Arabic: "prophet."

Nabi 'Isa ruh Allah: Arabic: "the prophet Jesus, God's spirit."

PLO: The Palestine Liberation Organization.

Quraish: An Arab tribe. Believed to be the tribe of Muhammad.

Qur'an (or Quran or Koran)*:* The holy book of Islam. The name means "that which must be recited."

Ramadan: An annual Muslim fast kept for one month, with fasting between sunrise and sunset.

Salaam: "Peace"—a conventional greeting in Arabic.

Salat: Muslim prayer.

Shahada: The Muslim creed.

Shahid: A martyr in Islam.

Shalom: "Peace"—a conventional greeting in Hebrew.

Sharia: The system of Islamic law, dating from the seventh century A.D. and covering all areas of personal and community life.

Slicha: The Hebrew word for forgiveness; "to be sorry" in conventional speech.

Sulcha: An Arabic term for a meeting for forgiveness and reconciliation.

Sura: A numbered section of the Qur'an.

Talmud: A collection of nonbiblical writings expounding the oral law of Judaism.

Tanzil: Arabic: "sent down." A name for the revelations recorded by Muhammad.

Tawrat (also "Thaura")*:* Islamic word for the Torah (the five books of Moses: Genesis, Exodus, Leviticus, Numbers, and Deuteronomy).

Yom Kippur: The Day of Atonement. A Jewish annual fast (Leviticus 23: 26-32).

Zabur: Arabic: "the Psalms."

Zakar: Islamic thanksgiving.

Zionism: The biblically inspired longing in the heart of all true Jews to return to their promised land.

GOYAM
FOR
G - D

Other Good
Harvest House Reading

GLOBAL PEACE AND THE RISE OF ANTICHRIST
by *Dave Hunt*

World peace seemed just a dream not long ago. But now it's almost a reality. Could this be the peace that Scripture says will lead to the end of human history—to the final conflict between Christ and Antichrist?

Noted author and researcher Dave Hunt pieces together world affairs and offers a biblical analysis of how these global events could be setting the stage for history's final conflict. Hunt powerfully emphasizes that the study of prophecy is meant to stir our love for Jesus into active passion and to enrich our lives as we await His return.

HOW TO STUDY THE BIBLE FOR YOURSELF
by *Tim LaHaye*

This excellent book provides fascinating study helps and charts that will make personal Bible study more interesting and exciting. A three-year program is outlined for a good working knowledge of the Bible.

AMERICA: THE SORCERER'S NEW APPRENTICE
by *Dave Hunt* and *T.A. McMahon*

Many respected experts predict that America is at the threshold of a glorious New Age. Other equally notable observers warn that Eastern mysticism, at the heart of the New Age movement, will eventually corrupt Western civilization. *Who is right?* Will we be able to distinguish between the true hope of the Gospel and the false hope of the New Age?

Dave Hunt and T.A. McMahon break down the most brilliant arguments of the most-respected New Age leaders and present overwhelming evidence for the superiority of the Christian faith.

A PROPHETICAL WALK THROUGH THE HOLY LAND
by *Hal Lindsey*

An authoritative guide to the mysteries and beauty of the Holy Land as seen by world-renowned Bible prophecy expert Hal Lindsey. Illustrated with beautiful photography, this book portrays the fascinating places where God's promises have been fulfilled down through the ages and where the most momentous events of all time will soon take place.

WHEN THE WORLD WILL BE AS ONE
The Coming New World Order in the New Age
by *Tal Brooke*

Today the pieces are falling into place for a worldwide transformation. In the not-too-distant future a New World Order, unlike anything the world has ever seen, could appear almost overnight. There is an emerging global consciousness that is either an incredible historical coincidence or is, in fact, part of a sophisticated plan whose beginnings can be traced to antiquity. Could this be the global reality predicted 2,000 years ago by a prophet on the Isle of Patmos?

Tal Brooke spent two decades intently exploring the occult. His quest ultimately landed him in the heart of India where for two years he was the top Western disciple of India's miracle-working superguru, Sai Baba. Tal is a graduate of the University of Virginia, and Princeton, and is a frequent speaker at Oxford and Cambridge universities.

PEACE, PROSPERITY AND
THE COMING HOLOCAUST
by *Dave Hunt*

With fresh insight and vision, Dave Hunt dissects the influences that are at work to lull us into a state of euphoria and numb us to the reality of coming destruction. A startling account of the rapidly growing New Age Movement and the part it plays in the imminent return of Jesus Christ.

Dear Reader:

We would appreciate hearing from you regarding this Harvest House nonfiction book. It will enable us to continue to give you the best in Christian publishing.

1. What most influenced you to purchase *Islam, Israel and the Last Days*?
   - ☐ Author
   - ☐ Subject matter
   - ☐ Backcover copy
   - ☐ Recommendations
   - ☐ Cover/Title
   - ☐ _____

2. Where did you purchase this book?
   - ☐ Christian bookstore
   - ☐ General bookstore
   - ☐ Department store
   - ☐ Grocery store
   - ☐ Other

3. Your overall rating of this book:
   ☐ Excellent ☐ Very good ☐ Good ☐ Fair ☐ Poor

4. How likely would you be to purchase other books by this author?
   - ☐ Very likely
   - ☐ Somewhat likely
   - ☐ Not very likely
   - ☐ Not at all

5. What types of books most interest you?
   (check all that apply)
   - ☐ Women's Books
   - ☐ Marriage Books
   - ☐ Current Issues
   - ☐ Self Help/Psychology
   - ☐ Bible Studies
   - ☐ Fiction
   - ☐ Biographies
   - ☐ Children's Books
   - ☐ Youth Books
   - ☐ Other _____

6. Please check the box next to your age group.
   - ☐ Under 18
   - ☐ 18-24
   - ☐ 25-34
   - ☐ 35-44
   - ☐ 45-54
   - ☐ 55 and over

Mail to: Editorial Director
Harvest House Publishers
1075 Arrowsmith
Eugene, OR 97402

Name _____

Address _____

City _____ State _____ Zip _____

**Thank you for helping us to help you
in future publications!**